TRANSPORTATION INFRASTRUCTURE – ROADS, HIGHWAYS, BRIDGES, AIRPORTS AND MASS TRANSIT

ISSUES IN CRUISE SHIP SAFETY AND SECURITY

TRANSPORTATION INFRASTRUCTURE – ROADS, HIGHWAYS, BRIDGES, AIRPORTS AND MASS TRANSIT

Additional books in this series can be found on Nova's website under the Series tab.

Additional E-books in this series can be found on Nova's website under the E-books tab.

SAFETY AND RISK IN SOCIETY

Additional books in this series can be found on Nova's website under the Series tab.

Additional E-books in this series can be found on Nova's website under the E-books tab.

TRANSPORTATION INFRASTRUCTURE – ROADS, HIGHWAYS, BRIDGES, AIRPORTS AND MASS TRANSIT

ISSUES IN CRUISE SHIP SAFETY AND SECURITY

LEWIS D. RAINER
EDITOR

Nova Science Publishers, Inc.
New York

Copyright © 2011 by Nova Science Publishers, Inc.

LIBRARY OF CONGRESS CATALOGING-IN-PUBLICATION DATA
Issues in cruise ship safety and security / editors, Lewis D. Rainer.
p. cm.
Includes index.
Includes testimony originally presented before the Subcommittee on Surface Transportation and Merchant Marine Infrastructure, Safety and Security and the Subcommittee on Coast Guard and Maritime Transportation.
ISBN 978-1-61122-528-0 (hardcover)
1. Cruise lines--Safety measures. 2. Cruise lines--Security measures. 3. Cruise ships--Safety measures. 4. Cruise ships--Security measures. I. Rainer, Lewis D. II. United States. Congress. Senate. Committee on Commerce, Science, and Transportation. Subcommittee on Surface Transportation and Merchant Marine Infrastructure, Safety, and Security. III. United States. Congress. House. Committee on Transportation and Infrastructure. Subcommittee on Coast Guard and Maritime Transportation.
G550.I77 2010
363.12'3--dc22
2010041302

Published by Nova Science Publishers, Inc. † New York

CONTENTS

PREFACE

Cruise ships are the single largest passenger conveyances in the world, with one ship currently in service that can carry more than 8,500 passengers and crew. The Coast guard considers cruise ships to be highly attractive targets to terrorists, and according to a 2008 RAND Corporation report, cruise ships can represent high-prestige symbolic targets for terrorists. Additionally, in recent years, there have been increased incidences of sexual assault, theft and bodily injury aboard cruise ships. This book examines cruise ship safety and the potential steps for keeping Americans safe at sea

Chapter 1- Over 9 million passengers departed from U.S. ports on cruise ships in 2008, and according to agency officials, cruise ships are attractive terrorist targets. GAO was asked to review cruise ship security, and this chapter addresses the extent to which (1) the Coast Guard, the lead federal agency on maritime security, assessed risk in accordance with the Department of Homeland Security's (DHS) guidance and identified risks; and (2) federal agencies, cruise ship and facility operators, and law enforcement entities have taken actions to protect cruise ships and their facilities. GAO reviewed relevant requirements and agency documents on maritime security, analyzed 2006 through 2008 security operations data, interviewed federal and industry officials, and made observations at seven ports. GAO selected these locations based on factors such as the number of sailings from each port. Results of the visits provided additional information on security, but were not projectable to all ports.

Chapter 2- The association represents 24 cruise lines, whose vessels range in size from 50 passengers to 4,000 passengers. Their membership also includes 16,500 travel agencies and more than 100 business partners who provide a vast range of products and services to the cruise industry. These businesses are located throughout the U.S. and create thousands of jobs.

They have representatives and letters from the American Society of Travel Agents (ASTA), National Business Travel Association (NBTA), National Association of Cruise Only Agencies (NACOA) and the National Association of Commissioned Travel Agents. Each of these organizations attests to peoples' personal experiences with cruising and their views that it is a very safe experience.

Chapter 3- The author wishes to begin by asking you to imagine how you might feel if you had long saved and planned for a cruise vacation, and then had to abruptly end your voyage because you had been traumatized by a sexual assault while on the cruise. Specifically, imagine that for years you've put a bit of your salary aside each pay period to save up for your dream of a sunny cruise vacation with one of your close childhood friends. You have planned the trip in minute detail, after collaborating with your friend on which destination, what to bring with you on the trip, and which amenities you can afford.

Chapter 4- The contrast is stark. The cruise industry's insurance carrier states that sexual assault is a not uncommon problem, but the industry itself claims a cruise to be the safest form of commercial transportation. The industry's claim is grand – one which most passengers take at face value.

The Morgans (a pseudonym) took a cruise in 2005, never thinking twice about it being unsafe for their eight-year old middle daughter to go back to the family's cabin on her own. Along the way the youngster became confused and asked a crewmember in uniform for assistance. Instead of helping, the male (wearing a cruise line name plate) allegedly took the girl to a dark end of a corridor where there were no surveillance cameras and he masturbated in front of her. It was subsequently learned that the crewmember had previously worked for a different cruise line that had "do not rehire" marked on his personnel file. But he passed background checks and was hired by the current cruise line. It seems the cruise line also failed to notice that the name under which the man had applied for employment was different than the name on his personnel file.

Chapter 5- On September 19, 2007, at 11:00 a.m. in 2165 Rayburn House Office Building, the Subcommittee will meet to hold a hearing on cruise ship security practices and procedures. During a Subcommittee hearing in March 2007, entitled "Crimes Against Americans on Cruise Ships," representatives of the Cruise Lines International Association, Inc. ("CLIA") and the victims and family members of victims of alleged crimes on cruise ships agreed at the

Chairman's request to meet to discuss: (1) potential refinements in procedures for reporting alleged crimes on cruise ships to U.S. authorities; and (2) specific measures that could be implemented to improve the safety and security of passengers on cruise ships. These parties further agreed to re-appear before the Subcommittee to provide an update on the status of their discussions. This hearing is intended to receive that update and to examine whether the security practices and procedures aboard cruise ships are adequate to ensure the safety of all passengers.

Chapter 6- The Coast Guard is committed to improving the overall safety and security of the maritime transportation system. The cruise ship industry is a very important sector within this system. Each year, cruise ships around the world carry over eight million U.S. citizens as passengers. As I reported in March, nearly all cruise ships are foreign-flagged and subject to the exclusive jurisdiction of their flag State when operating seaward of any other State's territorial sea. Much of the alleged crime involving cruise ships is clearly under the jurisdiction of either a foreign coastal State or the cruise ship's Flag State, and therefore may not be within the jurisdiction of the United States. Determining whether the United States may have authority, jurisdiction, and resources to intervene in cases involving United States citizens aboard foreign-flagged vessels beyond the U.S. territorial sea is situationally-dependent, varying with timing and content of initial reporting.

Chapter 7- The author testified earlier this year that, after many months in development, in March 2007, the FBI, the U.S. Coast Guard and the Cruise Lines International Association (CLIA) reached an agreement on voluntary, standardized protocols for CLIA member lines to report allegations of serious violations of U.S. law committed aboard cruise ships. These reporting procedures are in addition to, but not in lieu of, the mandatory reporting requirements, e.g., the requirements of 46 Code of Federal Regulations (CFR) Part 4, or the requirements of 33 CFR Part 120. Further, this reporting does not replace or override any agency responsibilities and coordination mandated by the Maritime Operational Threat Response Plan.

Chapter 8- Today, the author has been provided with a unique opportunity to share my experiences surrounding the death of my father on board a cruise ship. I hope that my testimony will bring to light the necessity of viable safety practices and procedures to eliminate or at least minimize death, injuries and crimes at sea. The author is here today on behalf of his father, Richard Liffridge, who died on March 23, 2006 while taking what he believed to be a safe and enjoyable vacation on the Star Princess. In addition, the author am also representing the International Cruise Victims Association (ICV), which is an organization formed by grieving family members and victims who have unfortunately experienced preventable tragedies while on cruise ships.

Chapter 9- Thank you for your invitation to address you today about the continued prevalence of sexual assaults against Americans on cruise ships and the willful failure of the cruise industry to institute reasonable security measures, properly respond to sexual assault incidents, care for the victims of these horrific crimes, discourage an onboard culture of reckless profligacy, and warn future passengers of the ongoing danger of rape and sexual assault during cruise vacations.

Chapter 10- Thank you for your invitation to address you today about the continued prevalence of sexual assaults against Americans on cruise ships and the willful failure of the cruise industry to institute reasonable security measures, properly respond to sexual assault incidents, care for the victims of these horrific crimes, discourage an onboard culture of reckless profligacy, and warn future passengers of the ongoing danger of rape and sexual assault during cruise vacations.

In: Issues in Cruise Ship Safety and Security   ISBN: 978-1-61122-528-0
Editors: Lewis D. Rainer   © 2011 Nova Science Publishers, Inc.

Chapter 1

MARITIME SECURITY: VARIED ACTIONS TAKEN TO ENHANCE CRUISE SHIP SECURITY, BUT SOME CONCERNS REMAIN

United States Government Accountability Office

WHY GAO DID THIS STUDY

Over 9 million passengers departed from U.S. ports on cruise ships in 2008, and according to agency officials, cruise ships are attractive terrorist targets. GAO was asked to review cruise ship security, and this chapter addresses the extent to which (1) the Coast Guard, the lead federal agency on maritime security, assessed risk in accordance with the Department of Homeland Security's (DHS) guidance and identified risks; and (2) federal agencies, cruise ship and facility operators, and law enforcement entities have taken actions to protect cruise ships and their facilities. GAO reviewed relevant requirements and agency documents on maritime security, analyzed 2006 through 2008 security operations data, interviewed federal and industry officials, and made observations at seven ports. GAO selected these locations based on factors such as the number of sailings from each port. Results of the visits provided additional information on security, but were not projectable to all ports.

WHAT GAO RECOMMENDS

GAO recommends that the Commissioner of Customs and Border Protection (CBP), the unified border security agency in DHS, conduct a study to determine whether requiring cruise lines to provide passenger reservation data to CBP would benefit homeland security, and if found to be of substantial benefit, determine the appropriate mechanism to issue this requirement. DHS concurred with our recommendation.

WHAT GAO FOUND

The Coast Guard has assessed the risks to cruise ships in accordance with DHS guidance—which requires that the agency analyze threats, vulnerabilities, and consequences—and, with other maritime stakeholders, identified some concerns. Specifically, agency officials reported in January 2010 that there had been no credible threats against cruise ships in the prior 12 months, but also noted the presence of terrorist groups that have the capability to attack a cruise ship. The Coast Guard, cruise ship and facility operators, and law enforcement officials generally believe waterside attacks are a concern for cruise ships. Agency officials and terrorism researchers also identified terrorists boarding a cruise ship as a concern. The Coast Guard has also identified the potential consequences of an attack, which would include potential loss of life and economic effects.

Source: U.S. Coast Guard

Cruise Ship Escort by Coast Guard Boats

Federal agencies, cruise ship and facility operators, and law enforcement entities have taken various actions to enhance the security of cruise ships and their facilities and implement related laws, regulations, and guidance, and additional actions are under way. DHS and component agencies have taken security measures such as the Coast Guard providing escorts of cruise ships during transit, and CBP's review of passenger and crew data to help target passenger inspections. Cruise ship and cruise ship facility operators' security actions have included developing and implementing security plans, among other things. The Coast Guard is also in the process of expanding a program to deter and prevent small vessel attacks, and is developing additional security measures for cruise ships. In addition, CBP's 2005-2010 Strategic Plan states that CBP should seek to improve identification and targeting of potential terrorists through automated advanced information. CBP, however, has not assessed the cost and benefit of requiring cruise lines to provide passenger reservation data, which in the aviation mode, CBP reports to be useful for the targeting of passengers for inspection. GAO's previous work identified evaluations as a way for agencies to explore the benefits of a program. If CBP conducted a study to determine whether collecting additional passenger data is cost effective and addressed privacy implications, CBP would be in a better position to determine whether additional actions should be taken to augment security.

ABBREVIATIONS

CBP	Customs and Border Protection
DHS	Department of Homeland Security
IMO	International Maritime Organization
ISPS	International Ship and Port Facility Security
MTSA	Maritime Transportation Security Act
SAFE Port Act	Security and Accountability For Every Port Act of 2006
TSA	Transportation Security Administration

April 9, 2010

The Honorable Bennie G. Thompson
Chairman

Committee on Homeland Security
House of Representatives

Dear Mr. Chairman,

Cruise ships are the single largest passenger conveyances in the world, with one ship currently in service that can carry more than 8,500 passengers and crew. The Coast Guard considers cruise ships to be highly attractive targets to terrorists, and according to a 2008 RAND Corporation report, cruise ships can represent high-prestige symbolic targets for terrorists. Moreover, terrorists have either targeted cruise ships or been able to board cruise ships in the past. The hijacking of the cruise ship Achille Lauro and killing of passenger Leon Klinghoffer by terrorists in 1985 was a watershed event for the cruise industry, leading to major changes in cruise line security procedures. More recently, in 2005, a plot to attack Israeli cruise ships off of the Turkish Mediterranean coast was discovered after the premature explosion of a bomb that was intended for the attack. A successful attack on a cruise ship in or near U.S. waters that resulted in the closure of a U.S. port or discouraged cruise travel would likely harm the U.S. economy because of the significant economic impact that ports contribute to the U.S. economy. For example, in a 2006 report, the Congressional Budget Office estimated that the closure of the ports of Los Angeles and Long Beach would reduce the U.S. Gross Domestic Product by up to $150 million per day. Reduced demand for cruise travel following an attack could also have substantial economic effects as direct spending for goods and services by the cruise lines and their passengers in the United States was about $19.1 billion in 2008.

Enacted after the September 11, 2001, attacks, the Maritime Transportation Security Act of 2002 (MTSA) places much of the responsibility for coordinating and overseeing maritime security efforts with the Department of Homeland Security (DHS).[1] Within the department, the U.S. Coast Guard is the lead federal agency responsible for a wide array of maritime safety and security activities including those involving cruise ships and facilities. Other U.S. government agencies, such as DHS's U.S. Customs and Border Protection (CBP), the unified federal agency responsible for border security, support the Coast Guard's maritime security mission by addressing a wide range of issues that affect international maritime commerce, including screening passengers arriving in the United States by cruise ship. State and local governments and the private sector also have responsibilities to secure domestic ports.

You requested that we identify threats and vulnerabilities—two elements of risk—associated with cruise ships and the measures being taken to protect them.[2] This chapter responds to the following questions:

- To what extent does the U.S. Coast Guard assess risk related to cruise ships and their facilities in accordance with DHS's guidance, and what are the identified risks?
- To what extent have maritime security stakeholders taken actions to mitigate the potential risks to cruise ships and their facilities and to implement applicable federal laws, regulations, and guidance, and what additional actions, if any, could enhance cruise ship security?

To determine the extent to which the U.S. Coast Guard assesses the risks related to cruise ships in accordance with DHS's guidance, and determine the identified risks associated with cruise ships and their facilities, we reviewed relevant federal guidance on the use of risk management, including the National Infrastructure Protection Plan.[3] We also reviewed the Coast Guard's primary risk assessment tool, the Maritime Security Risk Assessment Model and Coast Guard documents describing the methodology and use of the risk assessment model. We analyzed the risk assessment model process and compared it to criteria with the risk assessment component of the National Infrastructure Protection Plan. We also analyzed the compiled nationwide results of the risk assessment model to determine the relative risks facing cruise ships and their facilities, as of July 2009. In addition, we interviewed Coast Guard headquarters personnel responsible for conducting comprehensive security reviews of critical maritime infrastructure with the risk assessment model, Coast Guard District personnel, and Coast Guard Sector personnel responsible for the implementation of the risk assessment model at the local level to discuss the relative risks in their areas of responsibility.[4] We interviewed Coast Guard, Navy, and private sector intelligence personnel actively engaged in determining possible threats to cruise ships and their facilities. We also interviewed Coast Guard and CBP officials; personnel from five state and local law enforcement agencies; security personnel from five cruise lines and the Cruise Lines International Association, the key international cruise industry association; security personnel from nine cruise ship facility owners and operators (and one port authority with some security responsibility for a cruise facility) to determine their perspectives on the vulnerabilities of cruise ships and their facilities. The Coast Guard and CBP officials were those responsible for cruise ship and facility security at both the national level and at the locations where we made site visits. Similarly, the law enforcement personnel we met with represented jurisdictions covered in our site visits, and we also interviewed the facility owners and operators at those sites. We made these visits to a nonprobability sample of six cruise ship ports in the United States and four Coast Guard Sectors.[5] We selected these locations based on the number of cruise ship sailings from the ports and the destinations for the cruise ship sailings. While the information we obtained from personnel at these locations cannot be generalized across all U.S. ports, it provided us with a perspective on the risks to cruise ship and facility security at the selected locations. The cruise lines we met with were primarily based on a nonprobability sample selected for their relative size and location. While their views may not represent views of all cruise lines, they do cover a substantial portion of the industry. For example, among members of the Cruise Lines International Association, the cruise lines we spoke with operate approximately 52 percent of vessels carrying 500 passengers or more in 2009.

To determine the extent to which maritime security stakeholders— including national and international governmental organizations, vessel owners, facility owners and operators, and law enforcement agencies—have taken actions to mitigate the potential risks to cruise ships and their facilities and to implement applicable federal laws and guidance, and determine what additional actions should be considered, we reviewed relevant federal legislation, regulations, and guidance. The scope of this review included MTSA; Security and Accountability For Every Port Act of 2006 (SAFE Port Act) amendments to MTSA;[6] pertinent implementing regulations—such as 33 C.F.R. Parts 101, 102, 103, 104, 105; the Coast Guard's Operation Neptune Shield operations order, Navigation and Vessel Inspection Circulars, and Maritime Security Directives, respectively. We analyzed data on the Coast Guard's security performance in meeting internal standards established for Operation Neptune Shield during fiscal year 2008, and on cruise ship and facility operator's security performance in meeting requirements identified in Coast Guard regulations, from 2006 to 2008. We found these data to be sufficiently reliable for the purpose of contextual or background information. To make this determination we conducted interviews with knowledgeable agency officials and performed data testing for missing data, outliers, and obvious errors. We also analyzed country reports from the Coast Guard's International Port Security Program—which has responsibility for assessing the antiterrorism measures maintained by foreign ports—and Port Security Advisories to determine the level of security at major cruise ship foreign destinations. Although we reviewed CBP's documents on passenger screening, such as the *Privacy Impact Assessment for the Automated Targeting System* and the *CBP Vessel APIS Guide*, and reviewed CBP's objective to improve its identification and targeting of potential terrorists as stated in its 2005-2010 Strategic Plan, we did not conduct an independent evaluation of the Automated Targeting System. We also reviewed a prior GAO report discussing the use of program evaluations to identify benefits of federal programs. We interviewed federal officials from various agencies, including the Coast Guard and CBP to discuss their actions to reduce risks to cruise ships and their facilities. We observed security activities and interviewed state and local law enforcement personnel and security personnel responsible for protecting cruise ships and their facilities from terrorist attacks at the ports we visited. While our observations at these locations cannot be generalized across all U.S. ports, it provided us with a general overview and perspective on cruise ship and facility security at the selected locations. We also made a site visit to one foreign cruise ship port to observe possible security actions other than those used in the United States. We selected this port because it was one of the few foreign cruise departure ports with many cruises to U.S. destinations.[7]

We conducted this performance audit from January 2009 to April 2010 in accordance with generally accepted government auditing standards. Those standards require that we plan and perform the audit to obtain sufficient, appropriate evidence to provide a reasonable basis for our findings and conclusions based on our audit objectives. We believe that the evidence obtained provides a reasonable basis for our findings and conclusions based on our audit objectives.

BACKGROUND

Cruise Industry Carries Many Passengers and Has Numerous Sailings from U.S. Ports

According to the Department of Transportation's Maritime Administration, over 9.3 million passengers departed from a U.S. port on North American cruises in 2008, on a total of almost 3,900 cruises from 30 ports.[8] The U.S. ports with the most departures were located in Florida and include Miami, Fort Lauderdale, and Port Canaveral. Other ports with over 150 cruise departures in 2008 include Los Angeles, Long Beach, San Juan, and the New York City area. The Western Caribbean—including islands west of Haiti and ports in Mexico, Central America, and Columbia—was the most popular destination for passengers in 2008. These cruises carried nearly twice as many passengers, or more, than any other destination. Alaska, the Bahamas, the Eastern Caribbean, and the Pacific coast of Mexico were other popular destinations in 2008. See figure 1 for a map showing leading North American cruise departure and destination ports, as well as the number of departing passengers for these ports.

Many Stakeholders Involved in Securing Cruise Ship Operations

Numerous international and domestic organizations play a role in the security of cruise ships. The non-U.S. stakeholders are diverse and have wide-ranging roles and responsibilities. These stakeholders include international organizations, governments of nations where cruise ships make stops or are registered, and owners and operators of the vessels and facilities (see table 1).

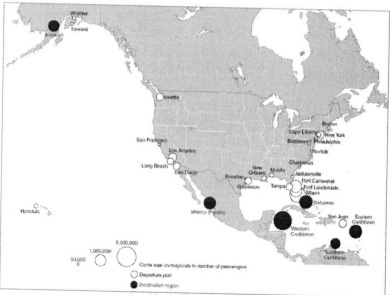

Sources: GAO analysis of US Customs and Border Patrol data; cruise line data; and the Official Steamship Guide International.

Figure 1. Leading U.S. Departure Ports and Destinations for North American Cruises in 2008.

Table 1. Key International Stakeholders with Maritime Security Activities

Organization or agency	Key maritime security-related activities
International organizations	
• International Maritime Organization (IMO) The International Maritime Organization is a specialized agency of the United Nations with 169 member states that is responsible for developing an international regulatory framework addressing, among other things, maritime safety and security.	• Responsible for developing and maintaining a comprehensive regulatory framework for shipping. • Responsible for developing international standards for port and vessel security.
• Cruise Lines International Association Cruise Lines International Association is composed of 25 cruise lines that represent 97 percent of the cruise capacity marketed from North America.	• Responsible for acting as the coordinating body and conduit of information for its members in meetings with U.S. security agencies at the national level.
Overseas governmental agencies	
• Designated Authorities Agencies of IMO member governments or their representatives responsible for implementing international maritime security requirements. In the United States, the designated authority is the U.S. Coast Guard.	• Responsible for setting security levels at a country's ports. • Responsible for reviewing vessel and facility security plans and overseeing compliance with these plans.
International private sector	
• Vessel owners, operators, and crew; and terminal operators	• Responsible for implementing vessel security plans that meet relevant security standards.

Source: GAO.

Table 2. Key Domestic Stakeholders with Maritime Security Responsibilities

Stakeholders	Key maritime security-related responsibilities
Federal government: Department of Homeland Security	
• U.S. Coast Guard	• Conduct vessel escorts, boardings of selected vessels, and security patrols of key port areas. • Ensure vessels in U.S. waters comply with domestic and international maritime security standards. • Review U.S. vessel and facility security plans and oversee compliance with these plans. • Meet with foreign governments and visit foreign port facilities to observe security conditions.
• U.S. Customs and Border Protection (CBP)	• Prior to a vessel arrival in the United States, screen information on its history, crew, passengers, and cargo for items that would lead to further examination. • Review documentation of all persons, baggage, and cargo arriving from foreign ports. Ensure that all have appropriate documents to gain access to the United States. • Take action to deny admissibility of aliens to the U.S., or take other appropriate enforcement action based on the results of the border search. • Operate the National Targeting Center that analyzes information used to target persons for additional screening.[a]
• Transportation Security Administration (TSA)	• Test technologies, practices, and techniques for passenger screening systems in the maritime environment.

Table 2. (Continued)

Stakeholders	Key maritime security-related responsibilities
	• Coordinate with the Coast Guard on security training and surge operations.
State and local governments	
• Law enforcement agencies	• Often act as land-based security for facility operators. • If agency operates a marine unit, support Coast Guard role through water patrols and possibly escorts.
• Port authorities	• Own many cruise ship facilities and responsible for ensuring their security.
Private sector	
• Vessel owners and operators	• Develop and implement vessel security plans that meet applicable laws and regulations.
• Security contractors	• Provide security services at cruise ship facilities.
• Facilities contractors	• Operate some cruise ship facilities on behalf of owners.

Source: GAO.

[a] The National Targeting Center is a multiagency operations center that conducts national level targeting and analysis in support of border-related efforts to identify and interdict terrorists through reports on individuals entering the country at land, sea, and airports.

In addition to international stakeholders, there are various domestic maritime security stakeholders in the United States. Table 2 lists key federal agencies and other domestic stakeholders, together with examples of the maritime security activities they perform.

Maritime Security Actions Are Guided by Legal and Regulatory Framework

International, national, and state and local requirements guide maritime security, including the security of cruise ships and their facilities. At the international level, the International Maritime Organization (IMO), through its International Ship and Port Facility Security (ISPS) Code, a part of the International Convention for the Safety of Life at Sea, lays out the international framework designed to help ensure maritime security.[9] National laws, regulations, and guidance direct federal agencies and vessel and facility operators on a nationwide basis. State and local requirements may also further direct activities of operators within their jurisdictions (see table 3).

The enforcement of security requirements aimed at vessels is governed by two different systems: flag state control and port state control. The flag state is the country in which the vessel is registered and flag state control can generally extend anywhere in the world that the vessel operates. A flag state that is a contracting government to International Convention for the Safety of Life at Sea has responsibility for ensuring that vessels flying its flag meet international security standards and that such flag state's standards be at least as stringent as those included in the convention's ISPS Code. The port state is the country where the port is located. Port state control is the process by which a nation exercises its authority over foreign-flagged vessels operating in waters subject to the port state's jurisdiction. Port state control is generally intended to ensure that vessels comply with various international and domestic requirements for ensuring safety of the port, environment, and personnel. Thus, when a foreign-flagged cruise ship enters U.S. waters or a U.S. port, the U.S. port state control program, administered by the U.S. Coast Guard, becomes an additional means of maritime security enforcement. According to an official of the Cruise Lines International Association, of the cruise lines included in our site visits, only one had a vessel registered in the United States. Hence, although they carry large numbers of U.S. passengers, the vast majority of cruise line-operated vessels generally come under U.S. authority only when they enter waters over which the United States has jurisdiction.

Table 3. Key International, National, and State Security Requirements Applicable to Cruise Ships

Promulgator	Law or guidance	Key provisions
International		
IMO	International Ship and Port Facility Security (ISPS) Code,[a] as implemented through Chapter XI-2 of the International Convention for the Safety of Life at Sea[b]	Sets out many of the international standards for vessel and port facility security. For example, all covered vessels shall have a designated security officer.
United States		
U.S. federal government	Maritime Transportation Security Act of 2002 (MTSA)[c]	Establishes a maritime security framework including many of the U.S. vessel and port facility security requirements and standards and for Coast Guard enforcement of many of such provisions. One such provision, for example, facilities and vessels that may be in a transportation security incident shall have vulnerability assessments.
	SAFE Port Act amendments to MTSA (2006)[d]	Sets additional requirements for Coast Guard regulation of port facility security. For example, at least one security inspection—an inspection of a facility to verify the effectiveness of its security plan—of regulated facilities shall be unannounced.
	Immigration and Nationality Act (1952)[e]	Section 235 of the Immigration and Nationality Act and implementing regulations provide for the examination of all persons seeking to enter the U.S. by a CBP officer. Once determined not to be a citizen or national of the United States the applicant will be inspected as an alien.

Table 3. (Continued)

Promulgator	Law or guidance	Key provisions
		All aliens are subject to inspection to determine the admissibility of all individuals seeking to enter the United States.
	Intelligence Reform and Terrorism Prevention Act of 2004[f]	Requires information about passengers and crews on cruise ships to be compared to watch lists to prevent suspected or known terrorists and their associates from boarding, or to subject them to additional security scrutiny.
Coast Guard	Implementing Regulations (such as 33 C.F.R. Parts 101, 104, and 105)	Based on legislative authority, set specific security requirements for U.S. flagged vessels and port facilities. For example, owners or operators of cruise ships shall ensure the screening of all persons, baggage, and personal effects for dangerous substances and devices.
	Operation Neptune Shield operations order	Sets internal Coast Guard standards for vessel (including cruise ships) security activities, which include escorts and security boardings—boardings performed to verify the information submitted in advance of the ship's arrival, verify that the ship and crew are operating as expected, and to act on intelligence that may have prompted security concerns. For example, Coast Guard units are required to escort a certain percentage of high capacity passenger vessels— those carrying 500 or more passengers—under different Maritime Security levels.[g] (Specific percentages are classified.)

Table 3. (Continued)

Promulgator	Law or guidance	Key provisions
	Navigation and Vessel Inspection Circulars	Provide guidance about the enforcement of or compliance with certain federal maritime regulations and Coast Guard maritime safety programs. For example, how Coast Guard inspectors are to ensure compliance with international safety and security standards on foreign cruise ships.
	Maritime Security Directives	Set security performance standards for stakeholders responsible for taking security actions commensurate with various Maritime Security levels. For example, one standard includes the various percentages of vessel stores that need to be inspected under different Maritime Security levels.
State Government: Florida	Seaport security legislation (2000)	At the state level, for example, Florida law requires the development and implementation of port security plans in Florida.[h]

Source: GAO.

[a] IMO Doc. SOLAS/CONF. 5/34 (Dec. 12, 2002). [b] 32 U.S.T. 47, T.I.A.S. No. 9700.

[c] Pub. L. No. 107-295, 116 Stat. 2064 (2002).

[d] Pub. L. No. 109-347, 120 Stat. 1884 (2006).

[e] Pub. L. No. 82-414, 66 Stat. 163 (1952).

[f] Pub. L. No. 108-458, 118 Stat. 3638 (2004).

[g] Maritime Security levels are a three-tiered threat warning system to provide a means to easily communicate preplanned scalable responses to increased threat levels. They are set to reflect the prevailing threat environment to the marine elements of the national transportation system, including ports, vessels, facilities, and critical assets and infrastructure located on or adjacent to waters subject to the jurisdiction of the United States.

[h] Fla. Stat. tit. 22 § 311.12(3).

Risk Management is Important for Cruise Ship and Facility Security

Risk management plays an important role in homeland security. Because the United States cannot afford to protect itself against all risks, Congress has charged DHS with coordinating homeland security programs through the application of a risk management framework.[10] In 2006, DHS issued the National Infrastructure Protection Plan, which is DHS's base plan that guides how DHS and other relevant stakeholders should use risk management principles to prioritize protection activities within and across each critical infrastructure sector in an integrated and coordinated fashion.[11] Updated in 2009, the National Infrastructure Protection Plan requires that federal agencies use this information to inform the selection of risk-based priorities and the continuous improvement of security strategies and programs to protect people and critical infrastructure by reducing the risk of acts of terrorism.

Within the risk management framework, the National Infrastructure Protection Plan also establishes baseline criteria for conducting risk assessments. According to the National Infrastructure Protection Plan, risk assessments are a qualitative and/or quantitative determination of the likelihood of an adverse event occurring and are a critical element of the National Infrastructure Protection Plan risk management framework. Risk assessments can also help decision makers identify and evaluate potential risks so that countermeasures can be designed and implemented to prevent or mitigate the potential effects of the risks. The National Infrastructure Protection Plan characterizes risk assessment as a function of three elements:

- **Threat:** The likelihood that a particular asset, system, or network will suffer an attack or an incident. In the context of risk associated with a terrorist attack, the estimate of threat is based on the analysis of the intent and the capability of an adversary; in the context of a natural disaster or accident, the likelihood is based on the probability of occurrence.
- **Vulnerability:** The likelihood that a characteristic of, or flaw in, an asset's, system's, or network's design, location, security posture, process, or operation renders it susceptible to destruction, incapacitation, or exploitation by terrorist or other intentional acts, mechanical failures, and natural hazards.
- **Consequence:** The negative effects on public health and safety, the economy, public confidence in institutions, and the functioning of government, both direct and indirect, that can be expected if an asset,

system, or network is damaged, destroyed, or disrupted by a terrorist attack, natural disaster, or other incident.

Information from the three elements that assess risk—threat, vulnerability, and consequence—can lead to a risk characterization and provide input for prioritizing security goals. For example, MTSA required the Coast Guard to prepare Area Maritime Security Plans for ports around the United States. These plans convey operational and physical security measures, communications procedures, timeframes for responding to security threats, and other actions to direct the prevention of and response to a security incident. In its regulations implementing MTSA, the Coast Guard gave the primary responsibility for creating the Area Maritime Security Plans primarily to the Captain of the Port, based on the Area Maritime Security Assessment.[12] Area Maritime Security Assessments examine the threats and vulnerabilities to activities, operations, and infrastructure critical to a port and the consequences of a successful terrorist attack on the critical activities, operations, and infrastructure at the port. Under the regulations, such assessments are to be risk-based, and assess each potential threat and the consequences and vulnerabilities for each combination of targets and attack modes in the area. With the information supplied in the assessment, the Area Maritime Security Plan is to identify, among other things, the operational and physical security measures to be implemented at Maritime Security Level 1 and those that, as risks increase, will enable the area to progress to levels 2 and 3.

THE COAST GUARD ASSESSES RISK TO CRUISE SHIPS AND FACILITIES IN ACCORDANCE WITH DHS'S RISK ASSESSMENT GUIDANCE; CONCERNS ASSOCIATED WITH WATERSIDE ATTACKS REMAIN

Risk Assessment

The Coast Guard uses a tool, known as the Maritime Security Risk Analysis Model, to assess risk for various types of vessels and port infrastructure, including cruise ships and cruise ship facilities, which is in accordance with the guidance on assessing risk from DHS's National Infrastructure Protection Plan. The Coast Guard uses the analysis tool to help implement its strategy and concentrate maritime security activities when and where relative risk is believed to be the greatest. The model assesses the risk—threats, vulnerabilities, and consequences—of a terrorist attack based on different scenarios; that is, it combines potential targets with different means of attack, as recommended by the risk assessment aspect of the National Infrastructure Protection Plan.[13] Examples of a Maritime Security Risk Analysis Model scenario related to cruise ships include a truck bomb or a boat attack. According to the Coast Guard, the model's underlying methodology is designed to capture the security risk facing different types of targets, allowing comparison between different targets and geographic areas at the local, regional, and national levels. Also in accordance with National Infrastructure Protection Plan, the model is designed to support decision making for the Coast Guard. At the national level, the model's results are used for (1) long-term strategic resource planning, (2) identifying capabilities needed to combat future terrorist threats, and (3) identifying the highest-risk scenarios and targets in the maritime domain. For example, Coast Guard officials reported that results are used to refine the Coast Guard's Operation Neptune Shield requirements for the number of required cruise ship escorts and patrols of cruise ship facilities. At the local level, the Captain of the Port can use the model as a tactical planning tool. The model can help identify the highest risk scenarios, allowing the Captain of the Port to prioritize needs and better deploy security assets. As we reported in March 2009, Intelligence Coordination Center officials stated that the Coast Guard uses the model to inform allocation decisions, such as the deployment of local resources and grants.[14]

Risk to Cruise Ships and Their Facilities

Although in January 2010 intelligence officials working at the National Maritime Intelligence Center stated there has been no credible terrorist threat against cruise ships identified in at least the preceding 12 months, stakeholders generally agreed that waterside attacks are a concern for cruise ships, and if attacks were successfully carried out, they could have extensive consequences. Despite the lack of evidence identifying recent threats, maritime intelligence officials identified the presence of terrorist groups that have the capability to attack a cruise ship, even though they have not identified any intent. As we previously reported in 2007, security officials in the U.S. government are concerned about the possibility of a future terrorist attack in a U.S. port.[15] For example, captured terrorist training manuals cite ports as targets and instruct trainees to use covert means to obtain surveillance information for use in attack planning. Terrorist leaders have also stated their intent to attack infrastructure targets within the United States, including ports, in an effort to cause physical and economic damage, and inflict mass casualties. In addition, as reported both by the Coast Guard and RAND, cruise ships have been terrorist targets in the past and are still considered attractive targets for terrorists.[16] Although intelligence officials reported that there have been no recent threats against cruise ships, this does not preclude the possibility of such an incident occurring in the future.[17]

According to maritime stakeholders, some concerns regarding cruise ship security exist, particularly with respect to waterside security. According to the Coast Guard's Strategy for Maritime Safety, Security, and Stewardship, one of the greatest risks associated with maritime scenarios is a direct attack using waterborne improvised explosive devices. Officials we interviewed from the Coast Guard's Intelligence Coordination Center stated that waterside attacks are a concern for cruise ships. Similarly, DHS's Small Vessel Security Strategy states that small vessels could be used as a waterborne improvised explosive device to attack maritime targets as they have in the past overseas.[18] The strategy further states that cruise ships operate in areas that are frequented by small vessels which may easily blend or disappear into other vessel traffic in ports and the coastal maritime environment, and are usually subject to less scrutiny than larger vessels in these areas.

Coast Guard personnel from all of the four Sectors and 18 of the 25 port security stakeholders we interviewed also stated that a waterside attack is one of the most significant concerns for cruise ships.[19] At one port we visited, various stakeholders responded to reports of a small vessel operating within the security zone of a cruise ship in 2007. Although the stakeholders cleared the cruise ship for departure after searching the area around the ship and its hull with divers, the small vessel was able to get within close proximity of the cruise ship before stakeholders responded. Representatives from the Cruise Lines International Association also reported that the greatest security concern for cruise ships is a waterside attack.

Waterside attacks can also occur while a cruise ship is in transit, such as when pirates in the Gulf of Aden and western Indian Ocean attacked cruise ships. For example, at least three cruise ships have been attacked by pirates on small boats while armed with automatic weapons and rocket propelled grenades. The three vessels were able to evade the pirates by either maneuvering or fighting back. Some cruise line officials we interviewed stated that they decided not to sail to places where security risks exist, but as of 2009, some continue to sail in the Gulf of Aden. One cruise ship operator we interviewed stated that the passengers who take cruises that sail in these areas tend not to be Americans and are people who are comfortable with risk. This official told us that they explain the level of risk to the passengers and their strategy for minimizing the risk.

According to officials at the National Maritime Intelligence Center there is also a concern that a terrorist could get on board a cruise ship to carry out a terrorist attack. For example, in 1985, terrorists were able to board and hijack a cruise ship, the Achille Lauro, resulting in the death of a passenger. Since that attack, various additional security measures have been implemented; including screening of passengers, crew members, and their baggage. However, according to a 2006 RAND report on maritime terrorism, if terrorists were successful in gaining access to a cruise ship, once on board, they could carry out various attack scenarios.

Coast Guard officials and some port security stakeholders reported that concerns also exist for cruise ship facilities at U.S. and foreign ports. Personnel from two of the four Sectors and 6 of the 25 port security stakeholders we interviewed mentioned a vehicle borne explosive at a cruise ship facility as a concern, and 5 of the 25 port security stakeholders we interviewed mentioned concern about the possible risk of an armed individual attacking others at a cruise ship facility.[20] Further, 6 port security stakeholders expressed concerns about the security level at some foreign ports, although Coast Guard reports from foreign port site visits indicate that there are few concerns with foreign ports that cruise ships typically call upon. Specifically, six recent reports from the Coast Guard's International Port Security Program[21] indicate that these countries, which include some of the most frequent cruise ship destinations, are generally found to be compliant with the ISPS Code. As part of the program's activities, the Coast Guard also recommends changes that could improve security at cruise ship facilities in some locations as a result of their visits to these locations. In addition, although the Coast Guard's October 2009 Port Security Advisory identifies 13 countries that are not maintaining effective anti-terrorism measures, a representative from the Cruise Lines International Association stated that these countries are not typical destinations for the cruise lines that the association represents.

A successful attack on a cruise ship could affect the ship, its passengers, and the U.S. economy. As a result of an attack, damage to the cruise ship could occur and the extent of the loss of life would depend on the severity of the attack, according to various studies.[22] Coast Guard officials stated that cruise ships are built to sustain various types of attack scenarios and keep passengers safe until they are able to be rescued, and that a very large hole in the hull would have to occur to cause any significant damage to the ship. Furthermore, according to the 2006 RAND study, most experts agree that sinking a cruise ship would be extremely difficult. However, according to this chapter and intelligence officials, the economic consequences of an attack on a cruise ship could be significant, as a successful attack on a cruise ship could result in decreased demand for cruise vacations, affecting a multibillion dollar industry. The RAND report further states that all attack modes targeting cruise ships have comparable estimates of potential economic harm. However, parasitic bombings—which involve a diver placing a highly explosive device on the hull of the ship, ramming attacks with improvised explosive devices, and biological attacks, including those involving contamination of a ship's food or water supply, are projected to present greater potential for human casualties.

STAKEHOLDERS HAVE TAKEN VARIOUS ACTIONS PURSUANT TO LAWS, REGULATIONS, AND GUIDANCE DESIGNED TO ENHANCE THE SECURITY OF CRUISE SHIP OPERATIONS AND ADDITIONAL ACTIONS ARE BEING CONSIDERED

Stakeholders' Actions

In their efforts to secure cruise ships and their attendant port facilities, the responsible stakeholders—including the Coast Guard, CBP, Transportation Security Administration (TSA), DHS, as well as cruise ship owners and cruise ship facility operators—have taken various actions to implement applicable key maritime federal laws, regulations, and guidance designed to help ensure the security of cruise ships and cruise ship facilities.

The Coast Guard conducts multiple types of security activities. The Coast Guard engages in both regulatory and operational activities designed to secure cruise ships and their facilities. As part of its regulatory activities, the Coast Guard inspects cruise ship facilities and cruise ships to ensure that they are meeting security requirements.[23] Under SAFE Port Act amendments to MTSA, the Coast Guard is required to conduct security inspections of MTSA-regulated maritime facilities, including cruise ship facilities, at least twice a year to verify the effectiveness of the facilities' security plans, and one of these inspections must be conducted without prior notice to the facility.[24] During our observations of two cruise ship facility inspections, Coast Guard inspectors reviewed the security plan, checked to ensure that guards were at designated access points, and questioned facility personnel on security procedures. See figure 2 for a photograph depicting a Coast Guard inspection of a cruise ship facility.

Source: U.S. Coast Guard.

Figure 2. Coast Guard Inspection of a Cruise Ship Facility.

In addition to the inspection of cruise facilities, to enforce security and safety provisions under international agreements, domestic legislation and Coast Guard guidance, the Coast Guard also inspects cruise ships entering U.S. ports.[25] Coast Guard guidance states that cruise ships are subject to security inspections as determined necessary by a risk-based targeting process to ensure that cruise ships are complying with security regulations and conventions.[26] Vessels that have not been inspected in the last 12 months are subject to an inspection upon port arrival under this targeting process. Coast Guard officials stated that security examinations on high-capacity passenger vessels can be both announced and unannounced. Coast Guard officials stated that there are systems in place to identify when cruise ships and cruise ships facilities are due for inspection.[27] Coast Guard officials stated that the Captain of the Port is responsible for ensuring that all cruise ship facilities inspections are conducted by reviewing the appropriate systems data. With respect to cruise ship inspections, Coast Guard officials stated that, at the time of our review, the agency exceeded the total number of required cruise ship security inspections. In February 2008, we reported that although Coast Guard officials told us that field units were meeting their inspection requirements for facilities, inspections may not have been documented in the Coast Guard's database, or inspections may have been delayed by staff being diverted to meet higher-priority needs.[28] Coast Guard officials stated that they are taking steps to rectify these issues by redesigning the database system to make it easier for the user to input data, which they expect to complete by 2011. In addition, they have created a daily report to inform local Coast Guard units when each facility is due for an inspection. Coast Guard officials stated that the agency is reviewing options on how to use its database as a method for headquarters to better track the local units' performance in meeting their inspection requirements.

The Coast Guard has also taken various operational actions designed to secure cruise ships. Through its internal guidance, the Coast Guard sets the standards for local Coast Guard units to meet for security activities, such as conducting passenger vessel escorts or security boardings. For example, Operation Neptune Shield requires Coast Guard units to escort a certain percentage of high capacity passenger vessels while in transit. These vessels include cruise ships, ferries, and excursion vessels carrying 500 or more passengers.[29] Coast Guard data on Operation Neptune Shield performance shows that some districts did not meet their requirements for high capacity passenger vessels escorts in fiscal year 2008; however, Operation Neptune Shield allows the Captain of the Port the latitude to shift resources to other priorities when deemed necessary, for example, when resources are not available to fulfill all missions simultaneously.[30] See figure 3 for a photograph of a Coast Guard boat escorting a cruise ship.

Another Coast Guard security action involves security boardings of cruise ships. Such security boardings are done to verify the information submitted in advance of the ship's arrival; verify that the ship and crew are operating as expected; and to act on intelligence. In 2008, the Coast Guard conducted pre-entry security boardings on some, but not all, cruise ships at major U.S. ports.[31] According to Coast Guard officials, these boardings were conducted because these cruise ships met certain criteria under the Coast Guard's targeting process.[32]

By regulation and at the discretion of the Captain of the Port, Coast Guard units, with or without the assistance of local law enforcement, may partake in other security measures as well. One such security measure is the enforcement of security zones that require other vessels to remain a certain distance from cruise ships. During our site visits to the ports, we observed the enforcement of security zones. See figure 4 for a photograph depicting a local law enforcement vessel enforcing a security zone at a port. The Coast Guard also partakes in waterborne, airborne, and shoreside patrols of critical infrastructure and key resources, including cruise ship facilities. In addition to its regulatory and operational activities to protect cruise ships and their facilities in the United States, the Coast Guard's International Port Security Program also reviews port security conditions in foreign ports and recommends actions and measures to improve the antiterrorism measures in use at such ports, pursuant to MTSA requirements.

Source: U.S. Coast Guard

Figure 3. Cruise Ship Escort by Coast Guard Boats.

Source: GAO.

Figure 4. Local Law Enforcement Vessel Enforcing a Security Zone.

CBP reviews passenger and crew lists for terrorist and criminal connections. CBP also maintains a role in the security of cruise ships and their facilities by screening passengers and crew for terrorist connections or criminal ties, and by helping to ensure that all passengers and crew are cleared for entry into the United States.[33] Under CBP's implementing regulations, operators of commercial vessels such as cruise ships are required to provide CBP with advance lists of information on passengers and crew—also known as a manifest.[34] Before a cruise ship departs or arrives in the United States, CBP checks these manifests to screen persons against certain databases, such as terrorist watchlists and the National Crime Information Center database, to determine their potential risk to the United States or the cruise ship. This screening process identifies individuals with potential terrorism links or criminal warrants, as well as identifies those passengers and crew with potential immigration admissibility problems, among other things.[35] For example, at one port we visited, we observed CBP officers removing a passenger from a cruise ship, due most likely to an outstanding criminal warrant, according to agency officials. For those cruise ships arriving in the United States, the agency also reviews the manifest to determine passenger and crew admissibility into the United States. Admissibility inspections are performed to determine the nationality and identity of each person wishing to enter the United States and for preventing the entry of ineligible aliens, including those thought to be criminals, terrorists, or drug traffickers. In the case of cruises originating at Canadian ports for U.S. destinations, CBP officials stated that CBP checks the admissibility of all passengers prior to the cruise ship departing Canada.[36] Finally, agency officials reported that they inspect all passengers and crew before they enter into the United States when they disembark cruise ships, including those passengers whom CBP inspected while in Canada.[37]

TSA primarily has a supporting role. TSA's role in cruise ship security is primarily as an advisor on transportation security screening and technologies. The agency also coordinates with the Coast Guard on security training and port security surge operations. TSA officials stated that the agency has conducted explosives and radiation screening technology pilot programs for passenger vessels and facilities, which include cruise ships, as part of its Security Enhancement and Capabilities Augmentation Program. Designed specifically for the maritime environment, TSA documents state that the program gives TSA the opportunity to network with different ferry and cruise ship operators around the United States, test emerging technologies, and develop strategies that the agency can use to respond to specific threats that arise from new intelligence or major events. Since February 2003, TSA officials stated that the agency has visited over 12 venues to test new technologies for screening passengers, ships, baggage, and stores to be loaded on passenger vessels, and that the goal of the pilot programs is to determine how the technologies work in different environments and in large scale application. The Security Enhancement and Capabilities Augmentation Program pilots can also provide operators with justification for grant funding, according to TSA. The pilots also give local agencies opportunities to observe and try the technologies. TSA officials stated that TSA shares the results of its pilots with the Cruise Lines International Association and cruise ship facility operators, including both pilot participants and nonparticipants. Although TSA does not track cruise ship facility operators that have implemented new technologies as a result of the TSA screening pilots, TSA officials reported that five facility operators, which included cruise ship operators, have adopted new technologies as a result of a TSA pilot program. TSA officials stated that TSA also creates and distributes security training courses for passenger vessel employees. The courses address topics to improve employees' security awareness, increase the effectiveness of their reactions to suspicious items and persons, and assist in their efforts to respond to a transportation security incident. According to TSA officials, the agency's involvement in surge operations is primarily through its Visible Intermodal Prevention and Response program. The program's deployments involve the use of the agency's assets, including explosive detection capabilities, transportation security officers, Federal Air Marshals and behavior detection officers—to help enhance the security of any transportation mode. Officials stated that since 2006 there have been 180 Visible Intermodal Prevention and Response maritime deployments.

DHS developed a strategy to address the small vessel threat. DHS released the Small Vessel Security Strategy in April 2008 as part of its effort to mitigate the vulnerability of vessels—including cruise ships—to waterside attacks from small vessels, and the implementation plan for the strategy is under review. According to the strategy, its intent is to reduce potential security and safety risks posed by small vessels through operations that balance fundamental freedoms, adequate security, and continued economic stability. The goals of the Small Vessel Security Strategy are to (1) develop and leverage a strong partnership with the small vessel community and public and private sectors; (2) enhance maritime security and safety; (3) leverage technology to enhance the ability to detect, determine intent, and when necessary, interdict small vessels; and (4) enhance coordination, cooperation, and communications between federal, state, local, and tribal stakeholders, the private sector, and international partners. Subsequent to the development of the strategy, DHS began drafting a plan to implement the goals of its strategy. In January 2010, a DHS official stated that the implementation plan was currently awaiting approval by the Deputy Secretary of DHS, after which it would need to be sent to the Office of Management and Budget for review. Subsequent to the Office of Management and Budget's approval, the implementation plan would be released. In September 2009, DHS's Office of Inspector General produced a report that identified concerns with the Small Vessel Security Strategy and the draft version of its implementation plan. According to the report, while DHS had made progress in responding to potential small vessel threats, more remained to be done to provide effective guidance and operate effective programs to address small vessel threats.[38] In addition, the Office of Inspector General recommended that DHS develop a more comprehensive strategy by (1) addressing the desirable characteristics and elements missing from its strategy and draft implementation plan and (2) evaluating the effectiveness of programs intended to support small vessel security before including them as part of its solution to improve security against the small vessel threats.[39] DHS partially concurred with the Office of Inspector General's first recommendation and plans to address this recommendation in the execution of its implementation plan. DHS did not concur with the Office of Inspector General's second recommendation to evaluate the effectiveness of programs intended to support small vessel security, stating that the agencies that submitted specific actions for the implementation plan had already considered their effectiveness to support small vessel security.

Cruise ship and facility operators implemented various security actions on board cruise ships and at facilities. Pursuant to the ISPS Code and its guidance, and Coast Guard's implementing MTSA regulations and guidance like other regulated vessels and facilities, cruise ship and cruise ship facility operators must develop and implement security plans that address vulnerabilities identified in their security assessments. ISPS-regulated cruise ship and cruise ship facility operators are also required to ensure security assessments are completed and inspections are conducted to ensure they are meeting security requirements. Under Coast Guard regulations specifically directed to cruise ship facility operators, cruise ship facilities must meet additional security requirements, such as implementing measures to screen all persons, bags, and personal effects for dangerous substances and devices; check the identification of all persons trying to enter the facility; designate holding, waiting, or embarkation areas within the facility's secure area to segregate screened persons and their personal effects from unscreened persons and their personal effects; and provide additional security personnel to designated holding, waiting, or embarkation areas within the facility's secure area, among other things. Similarly, cruise ship operators, under Coast Guard regulations specifically directed to cruise ships, must also meet additional security requirements, including the screening of all persons, bags, and personal effects for dangerous substances and devices; checking the identification of all persons attempting to board the cruise ship; and performing security patrols. To address such requirements in their security plans, stakeholders reported using various measures such as the presence of security guards or local law enforcement, and the use of cameras, vehicle checkpoints, canines, access control measures, and dive teams.[40] See figure 5 for a photograph depicting truck unloading areas and canine screening of stores to be loaded onto a cruise ship. Cruise ship and cruise ship facility operators may use local law enforcement and security contractors to help meet security requirements. We also observed security contractors conducting passenger screening and noted the presence of local law enforcement at the facilities during a port visit.

Source: GAO

Figure 5. Truck Unloading Areas and Canine Screening of Stores Awaiting Loading on Cruise Ship.

Although the Coast Guard has identified security-related deficiencies for cruise ship facilities and cruise ships, agency officials stated that cruise ship and cruise ship facility operators generally maintain good security measures. Of the over 1,900 cruise ship facility inspections the Coast Guard conducted in calendar years 2006 through 2008, Coast Guard data show 347 deficiencies recorded for all cruise ship facilities.[41] Coast Guard officials stated that cruise ship facilities tend to have more requirements than other types of port facilities but also tend to better implement security measures, and that most deficiencies are corrected at the time of the inspection.[42] Officials further stated that there was a decline in the number of cruise ship facility deficiencies in 2008, indicating that these facility operators have a better understanding of SAFE Port Act requirements. Personnel from the four Sectors we met with had issued few enforcement actions against cruise ship facilities in 2008—with one of the four Sectors issuing three letters of warning against a cruise ship facility for concerns related to access control.[43] Of the over 1,500 foreign cruise ship vessel inspections the Coast Guard conducted in calendar years 2006 through 2008, Coast Guard data shows 18 security-related deficiencies for foreign cruise ship operators. Violations were generally related to issues with the cruise ship's access control or restricted areas. Coast Guard officials stated that cruise ship vessel deficiencies tend to be less significant than those for other vessel types, and attributed this to the seriousness in which cruise ship operators approach security and the fact that these operators have a professional staff dedicated to security duties. Officials we interviewed from the four Coast Guard Sectors we visited stated that they had not issued any enforcement actions against a cruise ship in 2008, although personnel from one Sector stated that it had to delay a cruise ship because of a document violation.

Furthermore, federal officials and cruise ship operators we interviewed reported that cruise lines implemented security measures beyond what is required of them. Federal officials, including Coast Guard officials, told us that because of the significant impact that a cruise ship attack could have on the industry, the cruise lines are very serious about security. The five cruise ship operators we interviewed all stated that their daily security operations are comparable to what the Coast Guard requires at elevated threat levels. According to cruise ship operators, the actions taken by cruise ship operators to ensure security include making risk-based decisions regarding which ports to call on, whether to conduct additional screening on board ships at foreign ports, whether to require foreign governments to take additional actions to secure their ports, and providing their own security protocols at their private ports of call. Specifically, cruise ship operators stated that they have cancelled planned destinations because of security conditions in some locations. According to these operators, these decisions have been triggered by various factors such as the heightened security concerns following the November 2008 terrorist attack in Mumbai, India, piracy activity in the Gulf of Aden, and intelligence reports.

Stakeholders reported using various coordination efforts. As part of their efforts to secure cruise ships and their facilities, representatives from the Coast Guard, Cruise Lines International Association, and other port security stakeholders reported using various coordination efforts including meetings, jointly operated command centers, and the Coast Guard's HOMEPORT—a secure Internet communications portal between Coast Guard Sectors and the port stakeholders in their areas of responsibility. Specifically, stakeholders reported participating in the Area Maritime Security Committee meetings, security officer meetings, and Cruise Lines International Association security meetings[44] According to Cruise Lines International Association representatives, the association has hosted regular security meetings every 60 days for over 10 years, and coordinates with several intelligence agencies for these meetings, including the Federal Bureau of Investigation, Office of Naval Intelligence, the Department of State's Overseas Security Advisory Council, Coast Guard, and CBP. Furthermore, Cruise Lines International Association representatives stated that most of the security directors for the cruise lines are former military or law enforcement officers, who bring established contacts and relationships in the security and intelligence fields with them to the private sector. Personnel from all four Coast Guard Sectors and all 25 port security stakeholders we met with generally reported positive relationships among the stakeholders. Four of the 25 stakeholders, however, mentioned some challenges working with federal agencies. For example, 1 stakeholder stated that initially there was some uncertainty about who had authority to make decisions about cruise ship operations, the Coast Guard or CBP, but that it had become clearer over time.

Coast Guard Is Considering Additional Actions

The Coast Guard has plans to implement new maritime security awareness efforts to enhance the security of cruise ship operations. One of these efforts is intended to mitigate the threat posed by a small vessel attack. According to federal agencies, the U.S. government has limited information on recreational vessels, and it is difficult to detect a small vessel attack without prior intelligence. DHS documents state that the U.S. government has incomplete knowledge of the recreational boating public, their travel patterns, and the facilities they use, and that identifying and distinguishing legitimate small vessel users from those with intent to harm is difficult. Further, Coast Guard and Navy studies have demonstrated challenges in stopping a small vessel attack once one is under way. As we reported in March 2009, given the number of potential threats in many areas and the short period of time in which to respond to a threat, thwarting an attack by a smaller vessel without advance knowledge of the threat may prove challenging even with available systems and equipment that track smaller and noncommercial vessels in coastal areas, inland waterways, and ports.[45] According to one Coast Guard official, the ISPS Code contributes to the overall security of vessels but is not specifically aimed at preventing a small vessel attack. However, the Coast Guard provides armed interdiction capability that when present helps to deter small vessel attacks, according to this official. The concern about small vessel attacks is exacerbated by the fact that most cruise ships sail according to precise schedules and preplanned itineraries that are readily available through the Internet, advertising brochures, or travel agents. As a result, information that could provide valuable intelligence for terrorists is easily obtained, allowing an attacker to pick the time and place to prepare for and carry out an attack against a targeted cruise ship.

To address the waterside small vessel threat nationally, the Coast Guard has piloted a new initiative to enhance public awareness called Operation

Focused Lens. Operation Focused Lens is a Coast Guard District-level initiative to increase awareness of suspicious activity in and around U.S. ports. It complements Operation Neptune Shield by helping to identify, deter, and prevent a small vessel attack, and directs additional resources and effort toward gathering information about the most likely points of origin for an attack, such as marinas, landings, and boat ramps. A Coast Guard District official stated that Operation Focused Lens had minimal impact on cost and resources, as they were able to easily shift resources to meet the requirements of Operation Focused Lens. According to Coast Guard officials, the Coast Guard views Operation Focused Lens to be a best practice, and the agency is considering plans to integrate Operation Focused Lens into its community awareness program, America's Waterway Watch, and is developing requirements to implement aspects of Operation Focused Lens at additional locations. Coast Guard officials stated that they plan to discuss the expansion of Operation Focused Lens at the April 2010 Operation Neptune Shield conference.

The Coast Guard also plans to develop new security regulations for cruise ships by 2011 in response to recommendations regarding cruise ship security measures made by the National Maritime Security Advisory Committee in 2006. The advisory committee was established under authority of MTSA to provide advice to the Secretary of Homeland Security via the Commandant of the Coast Guard on matters such as national security strategy and policy, actions required to meet current and future security threats, international cooperation on security issues, and security concerns of the maritime transportation industry. In 2006, the Coast Guard asked advisory committee members to specifically review and make recommendations regarding cruise ship security measures. The advisory committee's recommendations included: (1) developing and publishing a listing of prohibited items not allowed on board cruise ships; (2) developing equipment performance standards for screening detection equipment; and (3) developing standards for screening operations, training, and qualifications of persons engaged in screening activities at cruise ship facilities.

Coast Guard officials stated that in an effort to address the National Maritime Security Advisory Committee's recommendation, a Notice of Proposed Rule Making for Cruise Ship Security Measures is under development with a publication date expected in 2011. Coast Guard officials stated the rule making will propose regulations that will provide detailed, flexible requirements for the screening of persons, baggage and personal items intended for boarding a cruise ship, and that they are working in consultation with TSA and the National Maritime Security Advisory Committee. Given the actions taken by the Coast Guard and port security stakeholders to protect cruise ships and their facilities from terrorist attacks, Coast Guard officials stated that aside from its planned actions, there are no additional measures that it should take or take more broadly at this time to protect cruise ships, as the current layered security practices included in vessel and facility security plans have successfully mitigated risks related to cruise ships and their facilities.

CBP's Collection of Additional Passenger Data Could Enhance Cruise Ship Security

Although CBP currently uses manifest data provided by the cruise lines as part of the screening process for cruise ship passengers and crew, CBP officials stated the agency's experience in the aviation context suggests that the routine collection and analysis of additional passenger data could enhance the agency's cruise passenger screening process. However, CBP is lacking full information on the benefit and cost of obtaining these data. Part of CBP's mission is to prevent terrorists and terrorist weapons from entering the United States, while also facilitating the flow of legitimate trade and travel. Under the Aviation and Transportation Security Act, air carriers operating flights in foreign air transportation to the United States are required to make Passenger Name Record information available to CBP[46] and under the agency's implementing regulations, CBP receives Passenger Name Record data in addition to manifest data for all passengers on international flights to or from the United States for purposes of ensuring aviation safety and protecting national security. Passengers provide data included in their Passenger Name Record to the airlines through the reservation process. Passenger Name Record data may include, among other things, a passenger's full itinerary, reservation booking date, phone number, and billing information, which is not usually available in the manifest data. According to CBP officials familiar with the process, Passenger Name Record data for airline passengers has been valuable because the additional information has helped the agency to better target passengers for inspection.[47] Specifically, the agency's National Targeting Center officials reported that airline Passenger Name Record data has allowed CBP to identify high risk passengers, including those who were not listed on watchlists—recognized by CBP as "previously unknown persons"—by (1) identifying links between passengers traveling with other high risk passengers or (2) identifying patterns of suspicious activity that have been identified with high risk passengers in the past. CBP provided examples of past efforts supporting the agency's view that the targeting of passengers for inspection through the use of Passenger Name Record data led to CBP taking adverse or enforcement actions, such as not allowing a high-risk passenger to board a flight. The examples indicate that CBP's targeting process identified passengers who represented various concerns, including terrorist-related concerns, as well as drug and immigration concerns. According to CBP, this process involved the use of Passenger Name Record data or the combination of this data with manifest data or other intelligence.[48] CBP officials also reported that Passenger Name Record data is provided to CBP earlier than manifest data, providing the agency with additional time to complete its passenger targeting process.[49]

CBP program officials reported that having access to Passenger Name Record data for cruise line passengers could offer benefits similar to those derived from screening airline passengers, although CBP has not conducted a study or evaluation measuring the benefits, or determining the potential cost to the agency, cruise lines, and cruise line passengers. Our previous work identified evaluations as a way for agencies to explore the benefits of a program.[50] In addition, CBP's 2005-2010 Strategic Plan states that the agency should seek to improve the identification and targeting of potential terrorists and terrorist weapons, through risk management and automated advanced and enhanced information. Furthermore, a January 2010 Presidential memorandum states that DHS should aggressively pursue enhanced screening technology, protocols, and procedures, especially in regard to aviation and other transportation sectors, consistent with privacy rights and civil liberties.[51] CBP does not require this information from all cruise lines on a systematic basis, although CBP reported that some CBP field units have access to some cruise lines' reservation systems and have received Passenger Name Record data on a case-by-case basis to enhance the information they have on passengers already identified for screening using other means. However, since field units do not have the same analytical tools as the National Targeting Center, they are less able to fully utilize the Passenger Name Record data on a systematic basis. CBP program officials stated that if the agency were to begin receiving and reviewing cruise line Passenger Name Record data, the effort would be highly automated and could allow for more effective and efficient targeting since the agency would receive the data earlier. Officials from CBP's Office of Information and Technology, however, stated that without specific requirements and further knowledge about the cruise lines' connectivity capabilities it is difficult to estimate the cost to both CBP and the cruise lines of implementing the technological aspects of a requirement to obtain Passenger Name Record data from the cruise lines. Based on CBP's experience with implementing such a requirement for the air carriers, CBP's Office of Information and Technology officials stated that there were costs to CBP and the air carriers for infrastructure, licensing, and ongoing maintenance; however, the cost depended on the air carrier's existing system and infrastructure at the time the requirement was being implemented. As of January 2010, CBP was spending about $3 million per year to maintain connections with most of the air carriers, and officials stated that creating and maintaining connections with cruise line reservation systems would require new infrastructure and costs.

According to a representative from the Cruise Lines International Association, the cruise lines would be willing to systematically share all Passenger Name Record data with CBP if required to do so. However, the Cruise Lines International Association did not know if this type of requirement would deter passengers from booking cruises. One cruise line official we interviewed stated that such a requirement would not be a major burden for their cruise line to implement, while another cruise line official stated that such a requirement could have significant cost implications for their cruise line depending on what data would be required and what requirements would be established for transmitting it to CBP, among other things.

In addition to assessing the impact that such a data requirement would have on agency and industry resources, other aspects of such a requirement, such as verifying the agency's statutory authority and assessing the impact on privacy issues, would also be important to study. Although CBP program officials stated that the agency's regulations for collecting Passenger Name Record data apply to passengers traveling on international flights and not passengers on cruise ships, CBP officials, including a representative from CBP's Chief Counsel, reported that various statutory authorities collectively provide the agency with the authority to require such information from the cruise lines. In addition, similar to the Passenger Name Record data requirement for air carriers, other important considerations for determining the cost and benefit of such a requirement for the cruise lines would be (1) assessing the privacy impacts of such a requirement on cruise passengers and developing any necessary public disclosure documents, and (2) determining the appropriate agreements that may be needed with other countries regarding the sharing and collection of this data. The Privacy Act of 1974[52] and the E-Government Act of 2002,[53] in general, require federal agencies to protect personal privacy by, among other ways, limiting the disclosure of personal information and informing the public about how personal data are being used and protected. The E-Government Act and implementing Office of Management and Budget guidance[54] require that agencies analyze how information is handled to (1) ensure handling conforms to applicable legal, regulatory, and policy requirements regarding privacy; (2) determine the risks and effects of collecting, maintaining, and disseminating information in identifiable form in an electronic information system; and (3) examine and evaluate protections and alternative processes for handling information to mitigate potential privacy risks.[55] Another privacy consideration would be the availability of a redress mechanism for individuals who felt that they had been unfairly denied boarding as a result of the screening process. As reported in DHS's 2006 report on Privacy and Civil Liberties, a robust redress program is essential for any federal program that uses personal information in order to grant or deny to individuals a right, privilege, or benefit.[56] DHS's Traveler Redress Inquiry Program serves as a single point of contact for individuals who have inquiries or seek resolution regarding difficulties they experienced during their travel screening at transportation hubs—like airports and train stations—or crossing U.S. borders. With respect to the collection of Passenger Name Record data from other countries, the privacy laws of other countries must also be considered. For example, in 2002, when air carriers operating international flights to and from the United States were first required to submit Passenger Name Record data to CBP, concerns about privacy were raised, and a permanent agreement on the sharing of this data between the United States and the European Union took several years to finalize. Without obtaining full information on the benefit and cost of requiring cruise lines to submit Passenger Name Record data to CBP and considering the associated privacy implications, CBP is not in the best position to determine whether the benefits of such a requirement would outweigh the potential costs to the agency and industry, and the risks to passenger privacy.

CONCLUSIONS

Given the number of passengers that travel on cruise ships each year and the attractiveness of these vessels as terrorist targets, it is important that the risk to cruise ships is assessed and actions are taken to help ensure the security of these ships and their facilities. Federal agencies and maritime security stakeholders, including cruise lines, have implemented various measures to better secure cruise ships and their facilities. As examples, the Coast Guard provides escorts for cruise ships to prevent waterside attacks and CBP screens passengers using manifest data to prevent terrorists from boarding cruise ships. Although these measures have been implemented and there has been no recent credible terrorist threat against cruise ships, this does not preclude the possibility of such an incident occurring in the future, particularly given the existence of terrorist groups that have the capability to attack a cruise ship. Moreover, the President's 2010 memorandum directing DHS to aggressively pursue enhanced screening efforts further underscores the potential importance of this type of security action. By conducting a study to determine whether requiring cruise lines to provide automated Passenger Name Record data on a systematic basis is cost effective and addresses privacy implications, CBP would be in a better position to determine whether additional actions should be taken to augment security through enhanced screening of cruise ship passengers.

RECOMMENDATION FOR EXECUTIVE ACTION

To enhance the existing screening process for cruise ship passengers, we recommend that the CBP Commissioner conduct a study to determine whether requiring cruise lines to provide automated Passenger Name Record data to CBP on a systematic basis would benefit homeland security, and if found to be of substantial benefit, determine the appropriate mechanism through which to issue this requirement. The scope of the study should include potential benefits to security, any need for additional authority and international agreements, resource implications for CBP and the cruise industry, privacy concerns, and any implementation issues related to the automated transfer of Passenger Name Record data from the cruise lines to CBP.

APPENDIX I: AGENCY COMMENTS

Homeland
Security

March 18, 2010

Stephen L. Caldwell
Director, Homeland Security and Justice Issues
U.S. Government Accountability Office
441 G Street. NW
Washington, DC 20548

Dear Mr Caldwell;

The Department of Homeland Security (DHS) appreciates the opportunity to review and comment on the Government Accountability Office (GAO) report, GAO-10-400: "*Maritime Security: Varied Actions Taken to Enhance Cruise Ship Security, but Some Vulnerabilities Remain*". DHS generally concurs with the report's findings and recommendation. We have provided our recommendation-specific comments below; technical comments have been provided under separate cover.

Recommendation #1: To enhance the existing screening process for cruise ship passengers, we recommend that the U.S. Customs and Border Protection (CBP) Commissioner conduct a study to determine whether requiring cruise lines to provide automated Passenger Name Record (PNR) data to CBP on a systematic basis would benefit homeland security, and if found to be of substantial benefit, determine the appropriate mechanism through which to issue this requirement. The scope of the study should include potential benefits to security, any need for additional authority and international agreements, resource implications for CBP and the cruise industry, privacy concerns, and any implementation issues related to the automated transfer of PNR data from the cruise lines to CBP.

Response: CBP currently receives PNR data from the airline industry, which has proven invaluable in identifying persons of interest, well in advance of their intended travel. To determine whether requiring PNR data would yield the same benefits in the commercial cruise environment, CBP will conduct a study that outlines the security, cost, and facilitation benefits an automated PNR system would bring to homeland security and the cruise line industry. Upon completion of the study, CBP will determine if the benefits of such a program are substantial enough to pursue full implementation of the program.

-2-

Again, we appreciate the opportunity to review and comment on this draft report and we look forward to working with you on future homeland security issues.

Sincerely,

Jerald E. Levine
Director
Departmental GAO/OIG Liaison Office

RELATED GAO PRODUCTS

Supply Chain Security: Feasibility and Cost-Benefit Analysis Would Assist DHS and Congress in Assessing and Implementing the Requirement to Scan

100 Percent of U.S.-Bound Containers. GAO-10-12. Washington, D.C.: October 30, 2009.

Maritime Security: Vessel Tracking Systems Provide Key Information, but the Need for Duplicate Data Should be Reviewed. GAO-09-337. Washington, D.C.: March 17, 2009.

Supply Chain Security: CBP Works with International Entities to Promote Global Customs Security Standards and Initiatives, but Challenges Remain. GAO-08-538. Washington, D.C.: August 15, 2008.

Maritime Security: National Strategy and Supporting Plans Were Generally Well-Developed and Are Being Implemented. GAO-08-672. Washington, D.C.: June 20, 2008.

Supply Chain Security: Challenges to Scanning 100 Percent of U.S.-Bound Cargo Containers. GAO-08-533T. Washington, D.C.: June 12, 2008.

Supply Chain Security: U.S. Customs and Border Protection Has Enhanced Its Partnership with Import Trade Sectors, but Challenges Remain in Verifying Security Practices. GAO-08-240. Washington, D.C.: April 25, 2008.

Maritime Security: Coast Guard Inspections Identify and Correct Facility Deficiencies, but More Analysis Needed of Program's Staffing, Practices, and Data. GAO-08-12. Washington, D.C.: February 14, 2008.

Supply Chain Security: Examination of High-Risk Cargo at Foreign Seaports Have Increased, but Improved Data Collection and Performance Measures Are Needed. GAO-08-187. Washington, D.C.: January 25, 2008.

Maritime Security: Federal Efforts Needed to Address Challenges in Preventing and Responding to Terrorist Attacks on Energy Commodity Tankers. GAO-08-141. Washington, D.C.: December 10, 2007.

Maritime Security: The SAFE Port Act: Status and Implementation One Year Later. GAO-08-126T. Washington, D.C.: October 30, 2007.T

Combating Nuclear Smuggling: Additional Actions Needed to Ensure Adequate Testing of Next Generation Radiation Detection Equipment. GAO-07-1247T. Washington, D.C.: September 18, 2007.

Information on Port Security in the Caribbean Basin. GAO-07-804R. Washington, D.C.: June 29, 2007.

Port Risk Management: Additional Federal Guidance Would Aid Ports in Disaster Planning and Recovery. GAO-07-412. Washington, D.C.: March 28, 2007.

Maritime Security: Public Safety Consequences of a Terrorist Attack on a Tanker Carrying Liquefied Natural Gas Need Clarification. GAO-07-316. Washington, D.C.: February 22, 2007.

Coast Guard: Observations on the Preparation, Response, and Recovery Missions Related to Hurricane Katrina. GAO-06-903. Washington, D.C.: July 31, 2006.

Maritime Security: Information Sharing Efforts Are Improving. GAO-06-933T. Washington, D.C.: July 10, 2006.

Cargo Container Inspections: Preliminary Observations on the Status of Efforts to Improve the Automated Targeting System. GAO-06-591T. Washington, D.C.: March 30, 2006.

Risk Management: Further Refinements Needed to Assess Risks and Prioritize Protective Measures at Ports and Other Critical Infrastructure. GAO-06-91. Washington, D.C.: December 15, 2005.

Homeland Security: Key Cargo Security Programs Can Be Improved. GAO-05-466T. Washington, D.C.: May 26, 2005.

Maritime Security: Enhancements Made, But Implementation and Sustainability Remain Key Challenges. GAO-05-448T. Washington, D.C.: May 17, 2005.

Container Security: A Flexible Staffing Model and Minimum Equipment Requirements Would Improve Overseas Targeting and Inspection Efforts. GAO-05-557. Washington, D.C.: April 26, 2005.

Maritime Security: New Structures Have Improved Information Sharing, but Security Clearance Processing Requires Further Attention. GAO-05-394. Washington, D.C.: April 15, 2005.

Cargo Security: Partnership Program Grants Importers Reduced Scrutiny with Limited Assurance of Improved Security. GAO-05-404. Washington, D.C.: March 11, 2005.

Maritime Security: Better Planning Needed to Help Ensure an Effective Port Security Assessment Program. GAO-04-1062. Washington, D.C.: September 30, 2004.

Maritime Security: Partnering Could Reduce Federal Costs and Facilitate Implementation of Automatic Vessel Identification System. GAO-04-868. Washington, D.C.: July 23, 2004.

Maritime Security: Substantial Work Remains to Translate New Planning Requirements into Effective Port Security. GAO-04-838. Washington, D.C.: June 30, 2004.

Homeland Security: Summary of Challenges Faced in Targeting Oceangoing Cargo Containers for Inspection. GAO-04-557T. Washington, D.C.: March 31, 2004.

Homeland Security: Preliminary Observations on Efforts to Target Security Inspections of Cargo Containers. GAO-04-325T. Washington, D.C.: December 16, 2003.

Maritime Security: Progress Made in Implementing Maritime Transportation Security Act, but Concerns Remain. GAO-03-1155T. Washington, D.C.: September 9, 2003.

Combating Terrorism: Interagency Framework and Agency Programs to Address the Overseas Threat. GAO-03-165. Washington, D.C.: May 23, 2003.

Nuclear Nonproliferation: U.S. Efforts to Combat Nuclear Smuggling. GAO-02-989T. Washington, D.C.: July 30, 2002.

Coast Guard: Vessel Identification System Development Needs to Be Reassessed. GAO-02-477. Washington, D.C.: May 24, 2002.

End Notes

[1] Pub. L. No. 107-295, 116 Stat. 2064 (2002).

[2] Risk assessment is a function of three elements: (1) threat—is the probability that a specific type of attack will be initiated against a particular target/class of targets, (2) vulnerability—the probability that a particular attempted attack will succeed against a particular target or class of targets, (3) consequence—the expected worst case or worse reasonable adverse impact of a successful attack.

[3] The National Infrastructure Protection Plan provides the unifying structure for the integration of critical infrastructure and key resources protection into a single national program. The plan provides an overall framework for programs and activities that are currently under way in the various industry sectors, as well as new and developing critical infrastructure and key resources protection efforts.

[4] Coast Guard Sectors run all Coast Guard missions at the local and port level, such as search and rescue, port security, environmental protection, and law enforcement in ports and surrounding waters, and oversee a number of smaller Coast Guard units, including small cutters, small boat stations, and Aids to Navigation teams. Coast Guard Districts oversee Sectors, other Coast Guard units, such as Air Stations, and major buoy tenders.

[5] Our site visits were to ports in Fort Lauderdale and Miami, Florida; Long Beach and Los Angeles, California; San Juan, Puerto Rico; and Seattle, Washington. The Sectors we visited were Los Angeles-Long Beach, Miami, San Juan, and Seattle.

[6] Pub. L. No. 109-347, 120 Stat. 1884 (2006).

[7] The ports we visited account for approximately 56 percent of all cruise ship passengers and approximately 54 percent of North American cruises in 2008.

[8] Destinations for North American cruises include Alaska, Bahamas, Bermuda, Canada/New England, Eastern Caribbean, Hawaii, Mexico, nowhere (a cruise that does not call on any ports before it returns to its departure port), Pacific Coast, South America, South Pacific/Far East, Southern Caribbean, Trans-Panama Canal, Transatlantic, and Western Caribbean and include a U.S. port of call.

[9] Adopted by IMO's Conference of Contracting Governments to the International Convention for the Safety of Life at Sea, the ISPS Code establishes requirements for contracting governments of countries where ports are located, contracting governments of countries

where ships are registered, operators of port facilities, and operators of vessels traveling on the high seas.

[10] For more information on how DHS and the Coast Guard utilized risk management for port security, see GAO, *Risk Management: Further Refinements Needed to Assess Risks and Prioritize Protective Measures at Ports and Other Critical Infrastructure*, GAO-06-91 (Washington, D.C.: Dec. 15, 2005).

[11] Critical infrastructure are systems and assets, whether physical or virtual, so vital to the United States that their incapacity or destruction would have a debilitating impact on national security, national economic security, national public health or safety, or any combination of those matters. Homeland Security Presidential Directive 7 divided up the critical infrastructure in the United States into 17 industry sectors, such as transportation, energy, and communications, among others. In 2008, under authorization of Homeland Security Presidential Directive 7, DHS established an 18th sector—Critical Manufacturing.

[12] The Captain of the Port is the Coast Guard officer designated by the Commandant to enforce within his or her respective areas port safety and security and marine environmental protection regulations, including, without limitation, regulations for the protection and security of vessels, harbors, and waterfront facilities.

[13] The Coast Guard Intelligence Coordination Center quantifies threat as a function of intent (the likelihood of terrorists seeking to attack), capability (the likelihood of terrorists having the resources to attack), and presence (the likelihood of terrorists having the personnel to attack).

[14] For more information on risk assessment models used in the aviation transportation mode, see GAO, *Transportation Security: Comprehensive Risk Assessments and Stronger Internal Controls Needed to Help Inform TSA Resource Allocation*, GAO-09-492 (Washington D.C., March 27, 2009).

[15] GAO, *Maritime Security: Federal Efforts Needed to Address Challenges in Preventing and Responding to Terrorist Attacks on Energy Commodity Tankers*, GAO-08-141 (Washington, D.C., Dec. 10, 2007).

[16] Reports that discuss a terrorist attack on a cruise ship include Michael D. Greenberg, Peter Chalk, Henry H. Willis, Ivan Khilko, and David S. Ortiz, *Maritime Terrorism: Risk and Liability* (Santa Monica, Calif., 2006); and United States Coast Guard, *The U.S. Coast Guard Strategy for Maritime Safety, Security, and Stewardship* (Washington, D.C., 2007).

[17] Although intelligence officials reported no credible threats against cruise ships, some stakeholders stated that they had experienced potential threats such as incidents involving false bomb threats, suspicious items, or the identification of a prohibited item on board a cruise ship.

[18] Department of Homeland Security, *Small Vessel Security Strategy* (Washington, D.C., April 2008). Additional information on the strategy is included later in this chapter.

[19] Of the seven stakeholders who did not mention waterside attacks, five reported either being comfortable with the level of law enforcement presence at their port or being more concerned about other threats, such as criminal acts of smuggling and drug trafficking at their port.

[20] These scenarios are not exclusive to a cruise ship facility, but rather any location where people are congregated.

[21] The International Port Security Program has responsibility for assessing the antiterrorism measures maintained by foreign ports. In response to MTSA provisions directing DHS to assess the effectiveness of antiterrorism measures maintained by foreign ports, which are served by vessels that also call on the United States, the Coast Guard established the International Port Security Program. A staff based in Washington, D.C. sets program policy and makes determinations regarding the effectiveness of antiterrorism measures. An operational element based in Portsmouth, VA and Liaison Officers in three regions (Asia-Pacific, Europe/Africa/Middle East, and Central/South America, for worldwide coverage) conduct country visits to review and discuss security measures implemented and share best

practices in order to assist other nations and facilitate bilateral exchanges. A Port Security Specialist Team based in Washington, D.C. was established to manage country visits to review and discuss security measures implemented and share "best practices." According to Coast Guard officials, during country visits, not all ports are visited by program officials.
[22] The Coast Guard has conducted studies on the impacts of different types of attacks on cruise ships, the results of which are classified.
[23] The Coast Guard performs other annual and periodic vessel inspections that are primarily focused on safety, during which security measures are also reviewed.
[24] Under Coast Guard guidance, a Coast Guard inspector must carry out the following steps in conducting a cruise ship facility inspection: (1) ensure the facility complies with the security plan; (2) ensure the approved security plan adequately addresses the performance-based criteria as outlined in federal regulations; (3) ensure the adequacy of the security assessment; and (4) ensure that the measures in place adequately address the vulnerabilities.
[25] Under Coast Guard guidance, the Coast Guard should determine if a cruise ship is complying with maritime security requirements through observation, asking questions, and reviewing security records. If there is evidence that the ship does not meet the applicable maritime security requirements, the Coast Guard can impose enforcement actions that include inspection, delay, or detention of the ship; restriction of ship operations; expulsion of the ship from port; and/or lesser administrative or corrective measures. According to Coast Guard guidance, a foreign flagged cruise ship's security plan is not generally subject to inspection, and the Coast Guard must obtain consent from the ship's flag state or the master of the ship before reviewing the ship's security plan.
[26] The Coast Guard utilizes a screening tool that promotes systematic evaluation of several risk factors related to a ship's compliance or noncompliance with domestic and international maritime security standards. The risk factors are: ship management; flag state; recognized security organization; the vessel's security compliance history; and the ship's last ports of call.
[27] For cruise ships entering a U.S. port, the Coast Guard uses a targeting system to determine whether the ship is required to receive an inspection. A Coast Guard database allows Coast Guard units to run a report on a daily basis for all facilities. The report highlights which facilities are due for an inspection.
[28] GAO, *Maritime Security: Coast Guard Inspections Identify and Correct Facility Deficiencies, but More Analysis Needed of Program's Staffing, Practices, and Data,* GAO-08-12 (Washington, D.C., Feb. 14, 2008).
[29] The required percentage of escorts changes at different threat levels. The Coast Guard can coordinate with local law enforcement to assist with meeting its Operation Neptune Shield requirements for escorting vessels.
[30] The Coast Guard collects Operation Neptune Shield data on all high-capacity passenger vessels, but does not separate the data by type of high-capacity passenger vessel, such as cruise ships or ferries.
[31] More specific information on the number of security boardings the Coast Guard conducts is considered security sensitive information.
[32] The Coast Guard uses a classified, risk-based tool to evaluate the security risk of a vessel entering into port, and determine whether a boarding is deemed appropriate. The tool helps Coast Guard units to determine the appropriate actions to be taken for a cruise ship, such as an inspection or boarding.
[33] Under the Intelligence Reform and Terrorism Prevention Act of 2004, for cruise ships on an international voyage that embarks or debarks passengers at a U.S. port, DHS is to compare information about cruise ship passengers and crew with consolidated database information relating to known or suspected terrorists and their associates.
[34] Under CBP regulations, cruise ships are required to transmit arrival manifest data at least 96 hours before entering the U.S. port or place for voyages of 96 hours or more; prior to departure of the ship from a foreign port for voyages less than 96 but at least 24 hours; or at

least 24 hours before entering the United States place or port for voyages of less than 24 hours. In addition, ships are required to submit manifest data 60 minutes before departure from the United States. Manifest data requirements include, among other things, full name, date of birth, gender, citizenship, country of residence, status on board the ship, travel document type, passport information (if required), address while in the United States (not required for U.S. citizens, lawful permanent residents, crew members, or persons who are in transit to a location outside the United States), voyage information, and ship information.

[35] In general, with respect to Coast Guard's maritime security regulations, the term "screening" is defined to mean "a reasonable examination of persons, cargo, vehicles, or baggage for the protection of the vessel, its passengers, and crew. The purpose of the screening is to secure the vital government interest of protecting vessels, harbors, and waterfront facilities from destruction, loss, or injury from sabotage or other causes of similar nature. Such screening is intended to ensure that dangerous substances and devices, or other items that pose a real danger of violence or a threat to security are not present."

[36] CBP officers conducting admissibility inspections for passengers boarding U.S.-bound cruise ships in Canada are permitted by informal agreement with Canadian authorities to check bags or do pat downs. However, according to Customs and Border Protection officials, taking any action beyond that would necessitate coordination with local Canadian law enforcement.

[37] Crew that are denied landing privileges by a CBP officer while in the United States are regularly mustered for compliance in the port of arrival and onward U.S. ports. CBP also notifies other federal and local law enforcement of detained crew for situational awareness.

[38] DHS Office of Inspector General, *DHS' Strategy and Plans to Counter Small Vessel Threats Need Improvement*, OIG-09-100, (Washington, D.C.: September 10, 2009).

[39] The Office of Inspector General report concluded that DHS incorporated two characteristics of an effective national strategy for combating terrorism—(1) purpose, scope, and methodology and (2) problem definition and risk assessment. However, the report stated that DHS had not fully addressed the remaining four characteristics—(1) goals, objectives, activities, and performance measures; (2) resources, investments, and risk management; (3) organizational roles, responsibilities, and coordination; and (4) integration and implementation.

[40] Under MTSA, a security plan for U.S. vessels and facilities must (1) be consistent with the requirements of the National Maritime Transportation Security Plan and Area Maritime Transportation Security Plans; (2) identify the qualified individual having full authority to implement security actions, and require immediate communications between that individual and the appropriate federal official and the persons providing personnel and equipment; (3) include provisions for—establishing and maintaining physical security, passenger and cargo security, and personnel security; establishing and controlling access to secure areas of the vessel or facility; procedural security policies; communications systems; and other security systems; (4) identify, and ensure by contract or other means approved by the Secretary of DHS, the availability of security measures necessary to deter to the maximum extent practicable a transportation security incident or a substantial threat of such a security incident; (5) describe the training, periodic unannounced drills, and security actions of persons on the vessel or at the facility, to be carried out under the plan to deter to the maximum extent practicable a transportation security incident, or a substantial threat of such a security incident; (6) be updated at least every 5 years; and (7) be resubmitted for approval of each change to the vessel or facility that may substantially affect the security of the vessel or facility. Under Coast Guard regulations, the Coast Guard is to review and approve security plans for U.S. flagged vessels and facilities. A foreign flagged vessel's security plan, under Coast Guard regulations, is generally not subject to Coast Guard review, approval, or inspection.

[41] Inspection data do not include domestic cruise ship facilities that typically cannot support a cruise ship as defined by MTSA. These facilities may handle gaming vessels or dinner cruises.

[42] Other port facilities include boat ramps, bulk liquid and oil facilities, and container facilities.

[43] A letter of warning is issued for minor first-time violations that operators take immediate action to correct.

[44] Area Maritime Security Committees established under Coast Guard's MTSA implementing regulations, in addition to the local Coast Guard Captain of the Port, may be composed of officials of federal, territorial, or tribal government; state and local government; law enforcement and security organizations; maritime industry and labor organizations; and other port stakeholders that either may be affected by security practices and policies or have a special competence in maritime security. The responsibilities of the committees include, in part, identifying critical port infrastructure, identifying risks to the port, developing mitigation strategies for these risks, and communicating appropriate security information to port stakeholders.

[45] GAO, *Maritime Security: Vessel Tracking Systems Provide Key Information, but the Need for Duplicate Data Should Be Reviewed*, GAO-09-337 (Washington, D.C., March 17, 2009).

[46] Section 115 of Pub. L. No. 107-71, 115 Stat. 597 (2001) (codified at 49 U.S.C. 44909(c)(3)).

[47] In November 2006, GAO issued a restricted report that discusses Passenger Name Record data. In May 2007, a public version of the report was issued. GAO, *Aviation Security: Efforts to Strengthen International Passenger Prescreening are Under Way, but Planning and Implementation Issues Remain*, GAO-07-346 (Washington, D.C., May 16, 2007).

[48] Detailed information regarding these cases is security sensitive information.

[49] CBP officials stated that there is always a concern about the accuracy and reliability of Passenger Name Record data for several reasons. First, this information is not standardized, that is, CBP receives Passenger Name Record data from 130 air carriers in about 100 different formats. CBP considers Passenger Name Record data as "dirty data" that requires great effort to process. Further, these data are collected or entered by the passenger or travel agent and there is the chance the data could be mistyped or a nickname could be used instead of a full name. CBP created algorithms in their system to account for similar names or acceptable misspellings to enhance the utility of the Passenger Name Record data.

[50] GAO, *Program Evaluation: Studies Helped Agencies Measure or Explain Program Performance*, GAO/GGD-00-204 (Washington, D.C., September 29, 2000).

[51] This memorandum was issued after receiving the conclusions of two reviews related to the attempt to bring down a Detroit-bound flight on December 25, 2009, by detonating an explosive device. The first was a White House-led review of the U.S. terrorist watch list system and the performance of the intelligence, homeland security, and law enforcement communities related to the attempted attack. The second review was led by DHS on technology and procedures used for airport screening.

[52] Pub. L. No. 93-579, 88 Stat. 1879 (1974).

[53] Pub. L. No. 107-347, 116 Stat. 2899 (2002).

[54] Office of Management and Budget, *OMB Guidance for Implementing the Privacy Provisions of the E-Government Act of 2002*, M-03-22 (Washington, D.C.: Sept. 26, 2003).

[55] The Privacy Act places limitations on agencies' collection, use, and disclosure of personal information maintained in systems of records, which are groups of personal information that are maintained by an agency from which personal information is retrieved by an individual's name or identifier. Among the act's provisions are requirements for agencies to give notice to the public about the use of their personal information. Also, when agencies establish or make changes to a system of records, they must notify the public by a notice in the *Federal Register* about the type of data collected; the types of individuals about whom information is collected; the intended "routine" uses of the data; the policies and practices regarding data storage, retrievability, access controls, retention, and disposal; and procedures that individuals can use to review and correct personal information. The E-

Government Act of 2002 requires agencies to conduct a privacy impact assessment when using information technology to process personal information.

[56] DHS, *Report on Effects on Privacy and Civil Liberties* (April 27, 2006).

In: Issues in Cruise Ship Safety and Security   ISBN: 978-1-61122-528-0
Editors: Lewis D. Rainer   © 2011 Nova Science Publishers, Inc.

Chapter 2

STATEMENT OF TERRY DALE, PRESIDENT & CEO, CRUISE LINES INTERNATIONAL ASSOCIATION, FT. LAUDERDALE, FLORIDA, BEFORE THE SUBCOMMITTEE ON SURFACE TRANSPORTATION AND MERCHANT MARINE INFRASTRUCTURE, SAFETY, AND SECURITY, HEARING ON "CRUISE SHIP SAFETY: EXAMINING POTENTIAL STEPS FOR KEEPING AMERICANS SAFE AT SEA"

INTRODUCTION

My name is Terry Dale. I am president and chief executive officer of the Cruise Lines International Association (CLIA), which has its headquarters in Fort Lauderdale, Florida.

My association represents 24 cruise lines, whose vessels range in size from 50 passengers to 4,000 passengers. Our membership also includes 16,500 travel agencies and more than 100 business partners who provide a vast range of products and services to the cruise industry. These businesses are located throughout the U.S. and create thousands of jobs.

We have representatives and letters from the American Society of Travel Agents (ASTA), National Business Travel Association (NBTA), National

Association of Cruise Only Agencies (NACOA) and the National Association
of Commissioned Travel Agents. Each of these organizations attests to
peoples' personal experiences with cruising and their views that it is a very
safe experience.

In the audience today is Bill Walsh, President of Cruise Travel Outlet,
who met with staff last week and shares a long affiliation with Massachusetts
and the cruise industry.

Travel agents like Bill Walsh are our front line partners. Travel agents are
among the very first to hear if there is a serious incident, or for that matter,
almost any kind of incident aboard a ship.

Bill readily acknowledges that the cruise industry has a 95 percent
satisfaction rating. In fact, in the 20 years he has been selling cruises, he has
never received a call from a passenger claiming to have experienced a serious
crime.

The purpose of this hearing is to examine cruise ship safety, and
specifically "potential steps for keeping Americans safe at sea."

This is an excellent subject, and many "steps" have already been taken. I
appreciate the opportunity to provide an update and address some of the
misunderstandings I believe exist.

I am pleased to be on a panel with Ken Carver, a member of CLIA's
Survivor Working group and a person I have had an ongoing dialogue
regarding cruise ship security. I am pleased that Evelyn Fortier of RAINN is
also on the panel. I have great respect for RAINN and the wonderful resource
that their association provides to victims of sexual assault. I look forward to
having a dialogue with RAINN.

The cruise industry's number one priority is safety of its passengers and
crew.

Quite simply, Americans are extremely safe at sea today.

In many ways, well documented by statistics and other evidence,
Americans are much safer in the well protected environment of a cruise ship
than they are on land.

Our industry has no higher priority –no stronger commitment– than to
maintaining our excellent record for the safety and security of all passengers.

Why, then, have these questions about safety even been raised?

I believe there are three principal reasons.

1. Our care and compassion in the past toward those who have suffered
    injury or loss has not always been satisfactory. We have made great
    strides over the past two years to improve our procedures, to provide

more support to those who have been injured or families that have been affected; and we are committed to continuing these efforts.

2. We are the only travel industry required by law to immediately report any serious incident or even allegation to federal authorities; in this case, the FBI and the U.S. Coast Guard.

3. When unfortunate incidents have occurred they typically receive far more publicity than comparable incidents in land-based settings.

There have been four House hearings on this issue, the most recent in September 2007 and since that hearing:

- We have held two more two all-day meetings with the working group of family members and their representatives to share and exchange ideas and recommendations. These meetings have provided a forum by which the families have heard directly from the FBI, the U.S. Coast Guard and the U.S. Attorneys Office. Our last meeting in Miami was held over several days and representatives of these agencies gave detailed briefings and answered many questions. The FBI also met with our group in November and discussed a new security training DVD that they were developing expressly for use by the cruise lines. Separately and during the Miami meeting the working group also addressed about 50 recommendations that had been put forward by the families.)

- Our major cruise lines now use the previously mentioned FBI-provided DVD for security training. The DVD offers FBI instruction on: initial response to a crime scene; securing a crime scene; crime scene photography and evidence collection.

- Two of CLIA's largest cruise lines have their security training programs certified by Lloyds Register, an internationally recognized security organization and a UK government program through Security Industry Authority.

- This spring CLIA sponsored the Family Assistance Foundation symposium in Atlanta, where a panel of survivors shared ideas and experiences with the audience.

- Our member lines' guest care programs have trained more than 1000 employees, bringing the total to date to more than 3000.

CRIME REPORTING

With respect to the reporting of such incidents, both the FBI and the U.S. Coast Guard have testified that the system is working efficiently.

Last September, Rear Admiral Wayne Justice, Assistant Commandant of the U.S. Coast Guard, testified to the House Subcommittee on Coast Guard and Maritime Transportation, and said: "We see no emerging requirement for legislative change regarding the incident reporting requirements."

He added that there were no known incidences of shipboard crimes going unreported.

Clearly, if the authorities were receiving reports from others that had gone unreported by the industry, the authorities would know this. As an aside, in this day and age of cell phones, camera phones and Wi-Fi cafes, the likelihood that a serious incident would go unnoticed, let alone unreported, would be very rare.

The House hearings also demonstrated that crime on cruise ships is extremely rare. Based on FBI reports from a six month period, the Coast Guard Subcommittee in it's September 2007 hearing memo noted that there were fewer than point zero one percent (0.01%) of passengers had been involved in a reported incident during that time period.

SAFETY AND SECURITY MEASURES

To give a sense of what these requirements mean in practice:

- Anyone boarding one of our ships is subject to more rigorous screening than is required for airline passengers at most of the world's airports.
- Every piece of personal luggage is strictly screened.
- Each cruise ship has embarkation and debarkation controls including biometric verification of all passengers and crew.
- All lists of passengers and crew are electronically submitted to U.S. authorities prior to departure from or arrival in the United States and screened against law enforcement databases.
- Each cruise ship has a qualified security officer and trained security staff whose duties are solely to provide onboard security for the

passengers and crew, as well as for the vessel itself. These security officers are experienced highly-trained professionals.

- Each cruise line also has supervisory security officers at the corporate level, usually ex-law enforcement, Coast Guard or military, in charge of managing fleet wide security and training of the vessel security officers.
- Every crew member is required and trained to look out for the security of all passengers.
- In addition, all major cruise lines now have trained staff to counsel and support families and individuals during emergency situations.

PASSENGER SATISFACTION

Independent surveys show that the vast majority of cruise passengers, 95 percent, say they are very satisfied with their cruising experience. Nearly 50 percent say they are extremely satisfied. And more than half of all passengers are repeats – cruising for the second or third or fourth time.

I submit that this would not be the case if safety or security were perceived as a serious problem. As the U.S. Coast Guard has testified, crimes onboard cruise ships are extremely rare.

I hope this background is helpful in assessing the level of safety and security for cruise ship passengers, despite the reports you may have heard of rare criminal activity, including sexual assaults, that have been widely reported, completely investigated, and yet sometimes exaggerated.

As an industry and as individuals, we deeply regret any such incident, and that in some cases, we have not provided sufficient support to the individuals or families affected. We have acknowledged this and over the past two years have worked closely with those families and their representatives and have welcomed their recommendations for improving our passenger services. Each of our large cruise ships now has specialized counselors.

Again the safety and security of our passengers is, has to be, and always will be our highest priority. We are constantly reviewing and improving our procedures.

Our position is that incident or crime of any kind is one too many.

MISLEADING STATISTICS

Regrettably, assertions are sometimes made and unofficial statistics are sometimes quoted that bear no relation to any known reality. I would like to try to clarify this point.

For example, at the September 2007 hearing of the House subcommittee, a witness stated that the rate of ship-board sexual assaults is twice the rate of those occurring on shore. The two figures serving as the basis for that statement, however, were shipboard sexual assaults and land-based forcible rapes. The difference between those two categories is significant because the definition of "sexual assault" includes behaviors such as the intentional touching of certain body parts through clothing. In addition, the FBI has confirmed that it does not even calculate the rate of land-based sexual assaults. Despite this key fact, the critics have continued to cite the FBI's statistics for "forcible rapes" that occur on land, mischaracterizing them as the (non-existent) land-based sexual assault rate, and misleadingly comparing them to the more broadly-defined "sexual assault rate" on ships. This is the basis for the false claim that a person is twice as likely to suffer a sexual assault onboard a ship as on land. We appreciate the opportunity to clarify the record on this important point.

CONCLUSION

In closing, let me say thank you again for conducting this hearing. We believe the record is clear – cruising is a very safe way to vacation, and our customer satisfaction levels, which are among the highest for any industry, would verify this fact – especially when placed along side the Federal data.

Our industry, as verified in previous testimony before the House of Representatives, is reporting all incidents – even allegations – and this reporting system is working well.

Our goal remains zero incidents and this industry works diligently every day to reach this goal. We have a very good record when it comes to passenger safety but we can always try and do more.

Passenger Safety is, AND WILL ALWAYS BE, our Number One priority.

Thank you.

EXECUTIVE PARTNERS

1 Priority Bicidal,
LLC Aker Yards
Amadeus North America, Inc.
American Association of Port Authorities (AAPA)
American Bureau of Shipping
American Guard Services, Inc.
Bahamas Maritime Authority
Bellcomb Technologies Bellegrove Medical Supply
The Berkely Group
BMT Group
Board of Commissioners of the Port of New Orleans
Business Research & Economic Advisors (BREA)
Chamber of Commerce and Industry of South Corsica (CCIACS)
Cruise Norfolk
Cruise Saint Lawrence The Coca-Cola Company
Ege Ports/Kusadasi Cruise Port
European Cruise Council Fidelio Cruise Software, Inc.
Fincantieri-Cantieri Navali Italiani S.p.A
Florida-Caribbean Cruise Association
Flamenco Marina
Fowler White Burnett, P.A.
Freeport Harbour Company
Fujiflim USA, Inc.
Gard
Germanischer Lloyd AG
Hayden, Miliken, Boeringer & hick PA
Halifax Port Authority
Hamilton, Miller & Birthisel, LLP
Hamworthy Water Systems, LTD
Hill, Betts & Nash, LLP
Hydroxyl Systems, Inc.
The Image Group
International Paint, LLC
Jacksonville Port Authority Jotun Paint, Inc.
Kaye, Rose & Partners, LLC
The Kezia Group
Lloyd's Register North America, Inc.

Maine Port Authority
Maritime Telecommunications Network/SeaMobile
Enterprises
Marseille-Provence Cruise Club
Marsh, Ltd.
Maryland Port Administration
Mase & Lara. P.A.
Massachusetts Port Authority
McAlpin Conroy, P.A.
McIntosh, Sawran, Peltz & Cartaya, P.A.
McRoberts Maritime Security, Inc.
MEIKO Marine
Metro Cruise Services, LLC
MEYER WERFT GmbH
MHG Services, Inc.
Milliken Carpet
Montreal Port Authority
NYCruise
On-Board Movies
Passenger Shipping Association (PSA)
Port Canaveral
Port Everglades Port of Galveston
Port of Houston Authority
The Port of Los Angeles
Port Miami
Port of Palm Beach
Port of San Diego
Port of San Francisco
Port of Seattle
Port of Shanghai
Port of Saint John
Ports America, Inc.
Quebec Port Authority
RINA S.P.A.
Royal Marine Insurance Group/RMTG
Seatrade Cruise Shipping Convention/CMP Princeton, Inc.
Steamship Insurance Management Services Limited (SIMSL)
Tampa Port Authority

The Port of Philadelphia and Camden, a Department of DRPA of PA & NJ

Throdon Bearings, Inc.
UK P&T Club
Unisource Worldwide, Inc.
Universal Marine Medical Supply
Vickers Oils
Wartsila
Wireless Maritime Services, LLP
World Cruise Industry Review

RESULTS OF RESEARCH

Satisfaction Levels with Various Vacation Alternatives

94.8% of cruise vacationers express total satisfaction with cruise experience. In comparison to other types of vacations, the two categories that generate the highest satisfaction levels are *all-inclusive resorts (46% extremely satisfied)* and *cruising (44%)*. However, the number of past cruisers (ever) more than doubles the number of all-. inclusive resort visitors (45% vs. 21 %).

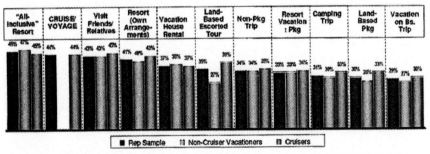

Q1. Overall, how satisfied were you with your vacation? Would you say you were extremely satisfied, very satisfied, somewhat satisfied, not very satisfied or not at all satisfied?

Level of Satisfaction with Types of vacations (01) % Extremely Satisfied (S-Point Scale; S = Extremely Satisfied)

ADDITIONAL CRUISE STATISTICS

Alaska

- Alaska embarked over 178,000 passengers in 2006.
- Almost 7,000 of Alaska's residents traveled on a cruise vacation in 2006.

Louisiana

- The Port of New Orleans embarked 72,000 cruise passengers in 2006.
- More than 85,000 of Louisiana's residents traveled on a cruise vacation in 2006.

Maine

- Ports in Maine embarked over 130,000 passengers in 2006
- Over 16,000 of Maine's residents traveled on a cruise vacation in 2006.

Massachusetts

- Operating on a seasonal schedule from April to November, Cruiseport Boston embarked over 62,000 passengers in 2006.
- Over 500,000 of Massachusetts' residents traveled on a cruise vacation in 2006.

Mississippi

- More than 30,000 of Mississippi's residents traveled on a cruise vacation in 2006.

New Jersey

- Cape Liberty embarked over 160,000 cruise passengers in 2006.
- Almost 322,000 of New Jersey's residents went on a cruise vacation in 2006.

Oregon

- Almost 60,000 of Oregon's residents traveled on a cruise vacation in 2006.

South Carolina

- Operating on a seasonal schedule from September-June, the Port of Charleston embarked over 105,000 cruise passengers in 2006.
- Almost 110,000 of South Carolina's residents traveled on a cruise vacation in 2006.

Texas

- The Port of Galveston embarked over 617,000 passengers in 2006.
- Almost 730,000 of Texas' residents traveled on a cruise vacation in 2006.

Washington

- The Port of Seattle embarked over 370,000 cruise passengers in 2006.
- Over 180,000 of Washington's residents traveled on a cruise vacation in 2006

*states represented by members of the Subcommittee on Surface Transportation and Merchant Marine Infrastructure, Safety, and Security

2006 NORTH AMRICAN CRUISE INDUSTRY ECONOMIC OVERVIEW

In 2006, the cruise industry continued to experience growth and its contribution to the U.S. economy. Direct purchases by the cruise lines and their passengers totaled $17.6 billion, a 9 percent increase over 2005. This spending resulted in $35.7 billion in total impact, an increase of 10 percent. The spending generated 348,000 jobs paying $14.7 billion in wages to American workers.

The more moderate rate of growth for the cruise industry in 2006 was attributed to a slower rate in capacity expansion and the overall decelerating growth of the American economy and consumer discretionary spending. However, more people than ever took cruise vacations.

In 2006, 12 million people worldwide took cruise vacations, a 7 percent increase over the previous year. Passenger carryings at U.S. ports also remained strong with 9 million embarkations.

U.S. ECONOMIC CONTRIBUTION OF THE NORTH AMERICAN CRUISE INDUSTRY IN 2006

Total economic benefit of the cruise industry in the United States	$35.7 billion
Direct spending of the cruise lines and passengers on U.S. goods and services	$17.6 billion
Total jobs generated by these expenditures	348,000
Total wages generated for U.S. employees	$14.7 billion

Cruise Industry Spending Benefits U.S. Industries

These economic benefits affect nearly every industry in the United States. Over 60 percent of the $35.7 billion in total gross output and 40 percent of the 348,000 jobs generated by the direct and indirect impacts of the cruise industry affected seven industry groups.

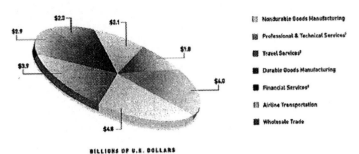

- Nondurable Goods Manufacturing
- Professional & Technical Services[1]
- Travel Services[2]
- Durable Goods Manufacturing
- Financial Services[3]
- Airline Transportation
- Wholesale Trade

MILLIONS OF U.S. DOLLARS

[1] Includes legal services, advertising, management consulting, engineering and architectural services and computer consulting services
[2] Includes travel agents, ground transportation services and U.S.-based excursions
[3] Includes banking, investment and insurance services

PASSENGER GROWTH AND VESSEL CAPACITY

Worldwide, 12 million people took cruise vacations in 2006, an increase of more than 7 percent, or 820,000 people, over the previous year. U.S. cruise passengers continue to be the large majority of the total worldwide cruise passengers, at 78 percent.

In 2006, a total of seven ships were added to the CLIA member line fleet, representing over 18,000 beds. This was the largest capacity increase since 2002. The industry's occupancy rate remained consistent at 104 percent.

U.S. Operating Statistics of the North American Cruise Industry

	2006	2005	2004	Annual Percentage Change 2006	2005
Capacity Measures					
Number of Ships	151	145	144	4.1%	0.7%
Lower Berths	249,691	230,891	225,714	8.1%	2.3%
Carryings (Millions)					
Global Passengers	12.00	11.18	10.46	7.3%	6.9%
Passengers Residing in the U.S.	9.36	9.06	8.31	3.3%	9.0%
U.S. Embarkations	9.00	8.61	8.10	4.5%	6.3%
Industry Spending in the U.S. ($ Billions)	$16.37	$14.99	$13.58		
Cruise Lines	$12.89	$11.76	$10.70	9.6%	9.9%
- Goods and Services	$11.08	$10.11	$9.36	9.6%	8.0%
- Capital Equipment (incl. net interest)	$1.81	$1.65	$1.34	9.5%	22.9%
Passengers and Crew	$3.48	$3.23	$2.88	7.8%	12.1%
Wages and Taxes Paid by Cruise Lines	$1.27	$1.19	$1.12	7.8%	6.0%
Total U.S.-Based Spending ($ Billions)	$17.64	$16.18	$14.70	9.0%	10.0%

US. Economic Impact of the North American Cruise Industry

U.S. PORTS LEAD THE WORD IN CRUISE EMBARKATIONS

The United States continued to increase its share of the global embarkations of the North American cruise industry during 2006, with U.S. ports handling 75 percent of all global cruise embarkations. More than 9 million cruise passengers began their cruises from U.S. ports, an increase of 4.6 percent from the previous year.

North American Embarkations by Port and Region*

Port	2006	2005
United States	9,081,000	8,612,000
Florida	5,018,000	4,843,000
Miami	1,876,000	1,771,000
Port Canaveral	1,396,000	1,234,000
Port Everglades	1,149,000	1,283,000
Tampa	457,000	408,000
Jacksonville	130,000	147,000
California	1,241,000	1,301,000
Los Angeles	592,000	615,000
Long Beach	378,000	363,000
San Diego	180,000	234,000
San Francisco	91,000	89,000
New York	636,000	570,000
Other U.S. Ports	2,286,000	2,098,000
Galveston	617,000	531,000
Seattle	373,000	337,000
Honolulu	318,000	236,000
Alaska	178,000	164,000
Cape Liberty	160,000	147,000
New Orleans	72,000	308,000
Boston	62,000	80,000
Baltimore	59,000	67,000
Houston	53,000	99,000
Philadelphia	52,000	50,000
Remaining U.S. Ports	242,000	79,000
Canada	423,000	655,000
Vancouver	402,000	635,000
Other Canada Ports	21,000	20,000
San Juan	155,000	581,000
North America	9,979,000	9,648,000
Rest of the World	2,021,000	1,852,000
Total	12,000,000	11,500,000

*All estimated cruise embarkations have been rounded to the nearest thousandth.

- Florida remains the center of cruising in the United States, accounting for nearly 56 percent of all U.S. embarkations. Port Canaveral and Tampa both increased embarkations by 12-13 percent over the previous year
- California's four cruise ports boarded more than 1.2 million passengers for their cruises, or nearly 14 percent of all U.S. cruise embarkations.
- 'Texas has been one of the highest growth markets, driven by an increase in embarkations at the Port of Galveston and development at the Port of Houston.
- New York boosted embarkations to 536,000 passengers, an increase of 45 percent, with the opening of the Brooklyn Cruise Terminal.
- Hawaii has increased its share of the cruise industry's impact in the United States with increased operations in 2006. Honolulu increased passenger embarkations by 34 percent.
- There were approximately 5 million visits at U.S. ports of call, primarily in Alaska, Hawaii and Key West

TOP 10 U.S. CRUISE PORTS BY EMBARKATION - 2006

The top 10 ports accounted for nearly 86 percent of all U.S. embarkations.

1. Miami	6. New York
2. Port Canaveral	7. Tampa
3. Port Everglades	8. Long Beach
4. Galveston	9. Seattle
5. Los Angeles	10. Honolulu

FAST FACTS

On average, a 2,000-passenger ship with 950 crew members generates approximately $322,700 in onshore spending in a U.S. homeport city (where passengers embark on their cruise).

Passenger data shows that 40 percent of embarking passengers stay one or more night in a port city pre- or post-cruise. On average, each overnight cruise visitor spends $289 per visit on retail, dining, local transit and lodging.

EVERY STATE BENEFITS FORM NORTH AMERICAN CRUISE LINE PURCHASES

The North American cruise industry benefited every state economy through $17.6 billion in direct purchases for goods and services for cruise operations. This direct spending in turn generated a total of $35.7 billion in economic impact and 348,000 jobs paying $14.7 billion in wages. States benefit from cruise line and port operations, the number of cruise passengers from their region and purchases of goods and services, such as air transportation, food and beverage, ship maintenance and refurbishment, engineering and travel agent commissions. The economic impacts were concentrated in 10 states that accounted for approximately 80 percent of the total U.S. impacts: Florida, California, Texas, Alaska, New York, Hawaii, Georgia, Washington, Illinois and Massachusetts.

STATE	DIRECT PURCHASES ($ MILLIONS)	TOTAL EMPLOYMENT	TOTAL INCOME ($ MILLIONS)	STATE	DIRECT PURCHASES ($ MILLIONS)	TOTAL EMPLOYMENT	TOTAL INCOME ($ MILLIONS)
Alabama	$100	1,785	$61	Montana	$5	91	$3
Alaska	$1,101	24,270	$927	Nebraska	$21	509	$19
Arizona	$181	3,495	$129	Nevada	$50	631	$23
Arkansas	$22	419	$12	New Hampshire	$43	504	$22
California	$1,194	44,703	$2,178	New Jersey	$321	5,442	$282
Colorado	$349	2,620	$135	New Mexico	$18	287	$10
Connecticut	$127	1,310	$77	New York	$1,086	13,421	$729
Delaware	$26	226	$10	North Carolina	$214	2,848	$108
District of Columbia	$38	153	$18	North Dakota	$8	158	$4
Florida	$5,847	125,104	$5,023	Ohio	$177	3,014	$126
Georgia	$667	9,288	$422	Oklahoma	$29	528	$19
Hawaii	$702	23,219	$675	Oregon	$78	2,689	$96
Idaho	$12	208	$7	Pennsylvania	$328	5,906	$254
Illinois	$442	6,398	$307	Rhode Island	$24	383	$13
Indiana	$249	3,769	$156	South Carolina	$70	1,430	$46
Iowa	$33	362	$12	South Dakota	$6	79	$2
Kansas	$52	2,211	$78	Tennessee	$59	993	$39
Kentucky	$58	893	$32	Texas	$1,120	19,351	$907
Louisiana	$128	2,224	$80	Utah	$53	832	$28
Maine	$24	379	$12	Vermont	$5	62	$2
Maryland	$148	2,139	$101	Virginia	$151	2,580	$122
Massachusetts	$387	5,657	$315	Washington	$631	16,300	$722
Michigan	$207	2,682	$123	West Virginia	$8	151	$5
Minnesota	$110	1,883	$89	Wisconsin	$50	882	$32
Mississippi	$27	394	$12	Wyoming	$3	40	$1
Missouri	$155	3,062	$126	U.S. Total	$17,643	347,965	$14,727

STUDY DETAILS

This analysis, conducted by Business Research and Economic Advisors (BREA), expands on a previous study from 2005. BREA gathered and analyzed data from a broad spectrum of the cruise industry, including all of the major cruise lines. The data has been aggregated and adjusted to develop industry-wide estimates of revenues and expenses. Additionally, BREA used its industry and macroeconomic models to trace the impact of cruise line spending on U.S. output and jobs by industry and used U.S. government impact factors to determine the state analysis.

The analysis provides a detailed outline of the study's conclusions regarding the cruise industry's revenues and expenditures in 2006. The full report may be viewed on the CLIA Web site at www.cruising.org.

Clia Member Lines

- American Cruise Lines
- Azamara Cruises
- Carnival Cruise Lines
- Celebrity Cruises
- Costa Cruises
- Crystal Cruises
- Cunard Line
- Disney Cruise Line
- Holland America Line
- Hurtigruten [formerly Norwegian Coastal Voyage)
- Majestic America Line
- MSC Cruises
- Norwegian Cruise Line
- Oceania Cruises
- Orient Lines
- Pearl Seas Cruises
- Princess Cruises
- Regent Seven Seas Cruises
- Royal Caribbean International
- Seabourn Cruise Line
- SeaDream Yacht Club

- Silversea Cruises
- Uniworld Grand River Cruises
- Windstar Cruises

Executive Partners

- 3M Marine
- ACS-Affiliated Computer Services
- Amadeus North America Inc.
- American Bureau of Shipping (ABS)
- American Guard Services, Inc.
- Avendra
- Bahamas Maritime Authority
- Barwil Unitor Ships Service
- Bellegrove Medical Supply
- Board of Commissioners of the Port of New Orleans
- Business Research & Economic Advisors (BREAI
- Cattenberg Engineering Inc.
- Campbell & Malafy
- Capital & Credit Financial Group
- Chamber of Commerce and Industry of South Corsica (CCIACS)
- Ege Ports/Kusadasi Cruise Port
- Fidelio Cruise Software Inc.
- Fincantieri-Cantieri Novell Italiani S.p.A,
- Fowler White Burnett P.A.
- Freeport Harbour Company
- Fuji Photo Film U.S.A., Inc.
- Gard
- Halifax Port Authority
- Hamilton, Miller & Birthisel LLP
- Hamworthy Water Systems LTD
- Hill, Betts & Nash LLP
- Hydroxyl Systems Inc.
- International Paint LLC
- Jacksonville Port Authority
- Jotun Paints, Inc.
- Kaye, Rose & Partners, LLP

- Lloyd's Register Americas Inc.
- Maine Port Authority
- Maritime Telecommunications Network Inc./SeaMobile Enterprises
- Marseille-Provence Cruise Club
- Marsh Ltd.
- Maryland Port Administration
- Mass & Lara, P.A.
- Massachusetts Port Authority
- McAlpin Conroy, P.A.
- McIntosh, Sawran, Peltz & Cartaya, PA
- McRoberts Maritime Security, Inc.
- MEIKO Marine
- Metro Cruise Services LLC
- MEYER WERFT GmbH
- MHO Services, Inc.
- Michael Stapleton Associates
- Montreal Port Authority
- NYCruise/New York City Economic Development Corporation
- On-Board Movies
- Ports America
- Port Canaveral
- Port Everglades
- Port of Galveston
- Port of Houston Authority
- Port of Miami
- Port of San Diego
- Port of San Francisco
- Port of Seattle
- Port of Shanghai
- Quebec Port Authority
- RNA S.P.A.
- RMIG Insurance*
- Seatrade Cruise Shipping Convention/CMP Princeton Inc.
- Steamship Insurance Management Services Limited
- Tampa Port Authority Teakdecking Systems, Inc.
- The Berkely Group
- The Coca-Cola Company
- The Image Group

- The Kezia Group
- The Port of Los Angeles
- The Port of Philadelphia and Camden - A Dept of the DRPA of PA & NJ
- Thordon Bearings Inc.
- UK P&I Club Unisource Worldwide, Inc.
- Universal Marine Medical Supply
- Vickers Oils Vitality Foodservice, Inc.
- Wartsila
- Wireless Maritime Services LLP
- World Cruise Industry Review

In: Issues in Cruise Ship Safety and Security   ISBN: 978-1-61122-528-0
Editors: Lewis D. Rainer   © 2011 Nova Science Publishers, Inc.

Chapter 3

TESTIMONY OF EVELYN FORTIER, VICE PRESIDENT OF POLICY, RAINN, BEFORE THE SUBCOMMITTEE ON SURFACE TRANSPORTATION AND MERCHANT MARINE INFRASTRUCTURE, SAFETY AND SECURITY, HEARING ON "CRUISE SHIP SAFETY: EXAMINING POTENTIAL STEPS FOR KEEPING AMERICANS SAFE AT SEA"

Mr. Chairman and members of the Subcommittee, thank you for scheduling today's hearing. This hearing is very timely, because high profile cases in which cruise passengers or crewmembers were raped, sexually assaulted, or disappeared continue to be reported. The safety of the nine or ten million United States citizens who take a cruise each year should be of vital importance to all of us; and the issue of cruise ship safety merits Congress' continued attention.

I want to begin by asking you to imagine how you might feel if you had long saved and planned for a cruise vacation, and then had to abruptly end your voyage because you had been traumatized by a sexual assault while on the cruise. Specifically, imagine that for years you've put a bit of your salary aside each pay period to save up for your dream of a sunny cruise vacation with one of your close childhood friends. You have planned the trip in minute detail, after collaborating with your friend on which destination, what to bring with you on the trip, and which amenities you can afford.

On the trip, a crewmember attired in a cruise security officer's uniform approaches you at the bar and questions you in a way you find unnerving. Hours later, this same crewmember knocks at the door of your cabin, which has no peephole, and, once you open the door to identify the visitor, he physically forces the door of your cabin open. He pushes you onto the bed in your cabin and rapes you. You reach out to other cruise line personnel, who enter your room and sit on the bed in which you were raped (thereby potentially contaminating the crime scene evidence). These cruise personnel suggest you collect any evidence you feel might be relevant and bring it to medical personnel on the ship. While you are coping with the life-shattering effects of having been raped, you later learn that the man who raped you was no security guard, but rather a janitor who filled in for the security guard.

Regrettably, this is how one American cruise line passenger described her experience during testimony before another congressional committee last year. And, unfortunately, hers seems not to be an isolated case. Numerous other United States citizens who have reported sexual assaults while on cruises described feeling helpless or virtually alone in the hours after they were victimized. If you are sexually assaulted while on a cruise vacation, you, like Laurie Dishman of Sacramento, California (the rape survivor described above) may find that any hope of your securing justice is extremely remote, perhaps even nonexistent.

WHAT CAN YOU EXPECT IF YOU ARE RAPED DURING A CRUISE VOYAGE?

The cruise industry is somewhat unique among businesses that provide services to U.S. consumers in that most cruise vessels sail under foreign flags and do not have to comply with many U.S. labor, environmental, or other regulations. The uniqueness of the cruise industry's situation, compared to many other businesses operated in the United States, becomes even more apparent when you compare the potential experience of an American rape victim at sea to the likely experience of an American rape victim on shore.

First, consider what happens after you are raped on land. You have the option to call the National Sexual Assault Hotline, 800-656-HOPE, toll free, any time of the day or night, or to visit the National Sexual Assault Online

Hotline at www.rainn.org, from anywhere in the country, through which you may immediately receive free and confidential online help from trained rape crisis personnel. Those who staff these hotlines are located at rape crisis centers around the country, and the availability of these services means you are not alone. Hotline staff and volunteers will provide you with immediate emotional support, and your local rape crisis center may offer to send their personnel to meet you and personally escort you to the nearest hospital or police station.

At the hospital, medical personnel can be counted on to evaluate you for injuries, take your medical history, and compile a rape kit containing DNA and other evidence. You also can expect that any DNA evidence collected during this examination will be sent to a crime lab for analysis, hopefully to be used later in identifying and prosecuting a potential suspect. The collection of DNA at this point in time preserves evidence for the future, for use in any later legal case. Protocols govern how this DNA is to be collected, analyzed, stored, and used in the criminal case.

If you immediately reported the assault to the local authorities, you can also expect that someone from a nearby police department will interview you and perhaps a suspect as well as any other witnesses. Your experience dealing with the criminal justice system ultimately may not be pleasant or result in your hoped for outcome, but along the way you can be fairly confident of certain things: that the police investigating the crime have the necessary jurisdiction to do so, that the police will preserve physical evidence for a possible trial, that certain local or state criminal laws will govern in your case, and that certain protocols will be followed in the police investigation. It's also within the realm of possibility that a local prosecutor will find your case deserving of prosecution and your predator is brought to justice. A victim advocate may be assigned to offer guidance and support to you along the way; also, you and your family members or close friends have the option of seeking counseling at your local rape crisis center, to assist in your long-term recovery.

If you, a U.S. citizen, are raped during a cruise, by contrast, your situation is potentially quite different, and you can be far less certain of what will happen next. Because most cruise ships are foreign-flagged vessels, because the perpetrator may be a foreign national, and because you may be in international waters when the assault occurs, you face a host of legal uncertainties. For example, you cannot automatically assume that certain laws will cover the incident, due to messy jurisdictional issues that arise in some of these cases.

Such uncertainties are in addition to your having to cope (far from home and absent your usual support network) with the emotional and physical consequences of having been assaulted. In the immediate aftermath of the assault, for example, you might not have a friend or family member traveling with you on board. You probably will not find any rape crisis personnel onboard to support you, let alone law enforcement officials to come to your aid on the ship.

If traveling alone, you might turn to cruise ship employees for help, only to later find that the cruise line has a vested interest in shielding themselves against negative publicity or legal jeopardy (and protecting such interests may come at the expense of your own interest in securing justice and getting appropriate medical care). If you were assaulted by a crewmember, and you are a passenger on the ship, you might have good reason to wonder how any security personnel hired by the cruise line will react if presented with any situation giving rise to a potential conflict of interest between their employer's legal situation and your safety.

You may encounter someone onboard who can competently and sympathetically explain to you what needs to happen in order for you to report the crime to the proper authorities and have the crime investigated. At this point in time, you probably have three options, each of which has certain drawbacks:

Option #1: Your first option is to disembark at the next port and report the crime to the local authorities on shore. There is a good chance you will not speak the same language as the local police and are unfamiliar with local customs. Perhaps no one told you that you should approach your nearest U.S. embassy or consulate for assistance, and you did not initially seek their help. You might learn later that, due to jurisdictional uncertainties, the authorities you approached do not have sole jurisdiction over your case, and that perhaps you should have reported the crime to authorities in an entirely different jurisdiction. (Alternatively, the local authorities may not want to assume responsibility for the criminal investigation if they perceive that the sexual assault occurred in international waters.)

If local authorities do decide to investigate, key evidence may have dissipated by the time you contact them. That's because, unless someone onboard assumed responsibility for immediately securing the crime scene, evidence may already have been contaminated or cleaned by others by the time the local police arrive. Also, before local authorities show up, the offender may already have either collaborated with others, or been dismissed by the cruise line and escorted off the ship. (If the offender then travels to another country, it will be difficult, if not impossible, to find them again).

Finally, even assuming the local investigation proceeds, and charges are brought against the perpetrator, you may face significant personal obstacles to cooperating with the prosecution. You may have to take time off from work and leave behind your friends or family in the United States to return again, perhaps more than once or for an extended period, to the foreign jurisdiction that is prosecuting the case. You may find, too, that you are completely unfamiliar with the legal system of that particular jurisdiction.

Option #2: The obstacles presented above may seem overwhelming, and so perhaps you are inclined to pursue a different course of action. Your second option as a victim of sexual assault would involve reporting the crime to the Federal Bureau of Investigation (FBI), in cooperation with the cruise line. But this option, too, has drawbacks for you, as the FBI can investigate crimes reported to it by the cruise lines, but typically would not be in a position to act as an onboard police force immediately after your assault.

The FBI typically will not board a ship to interview the victim or other potential witnesses to the crime until after the ship docks. In the meantime, here again, there is the risk that no one will assume responsibility for securing the crime scene or ensuring that potential witnesses do not collaborate or disperse. Once again, if the cruise line escorts the offender off the ship at the next port of call, or if the offender leaves, it may be difficult, if not impossible, to find them again.

It also is not certain that a cruise victim will receive adequate medical care or that trained personnel will be available to collect DNA or other evidence immediately following an assault. (Laurie Dishman, who reported being raped by a crew member while on a cruise in 2006, testified last year that ship personnel expected her to do the job of collecting any crime scene evidence herself. She also was asked to pay for her own rape kit, which would not have been the case had she gone to a hospital in the United States.)

Also, certain thresholds must be met for an FBI investigation to proceed and for federal prosecutors to bring charges. In the case of a sexual assault, for example, where the victim's consent is an issue, the case might not move beyond the initial phase of information gathering. The victim may find, after the FBI collects such information, that the chances of a federal prosecutor pursuing rape charges are extremely remote. The decision whether or not to prosecute the case lies with federal prosecutors; and these decisions are often made based on the severity of the crime, the likelihood of successful prosecution leading to conviction and, of course, available federal resources.

Option #3: For a victim of sexual assault, a third option is to disembark at the ship's next port of call, and take the next flight home. In the immediate aftermath of the crime, the victim may find this option the most appealing of the three, because it allows the victim to quickly escape the surroundings in which the assault occurred as well as the perpetrator, who may still be lurking somewhere nearby.

The victim may, however, later find — maybe years later — that the repercussions of having been raped continue to haunt him or her. Like many of rape's survivors, in the weeks, months, or years after the assault, a cruise victim of sexual assault may experience flashbacks, depression, nightmares, employment difficulties, or other negative effects and in some cases, even be suicidal. Any hope of securing justice – which is often important to victims in their recovery – may have disappeared if the victim did not formally report the rape while onboard and the cruise line declines to record the complaint once the cruise has ended.

Meanwhile, the offender gets a free pass to prey on additional victims.

WHAT IS YOUR RISK OF BEING ASSAULTED ABOARD A CRUISE?

According to FBI testimony at another congressional hearing in March 2007, sexual "[s]exual assault and physical assaults on cruise ships were the leading crime reported to and investigated by the FBI on the high seas over the last five years at 55 percent and 22 percent respectively." The FBI also noted, at a different hearing last September, that the cruise lines reported 41 instances of sexual assault[1] during a six-month period in 2007:

"Since April 1, the cruise lines have reported 41 instances of sexual assault. Of these 41 incidents, 19 represented allegations of sexual activity generally categorized as rape, three of which occurred on shore, and, thus, outside the jurisdiction of the FBI. Based on the 41 reports, the FBI opened 13 investigative cases. Five of these cases have been closed for reasons of victim reluctance to pursue prosecution or prosecutive declination from the United States Attorney's Office. Eight investigations are ongoing."

The cruise industry maintains that the rate of sexual assault at sea is significantly lower than the on shore rate of sexual assault. According to the cruise industry, during the three-year period from 2003 to 2005, when roughly 31 million North Americans sailed on cruise ships, there were 178 complaints of sexual assaults. But because data on rates of sexual assault during cruise voyages is not easily accessible to the public, it is difficult for us to evaluate the accuracy of such statistics.

We note that the industry's position is directly contradicted by the 2007 congressional testimony of Dr. Ross Klein, who suggested that the rate of sexual assault on board ships could be as much as 50 percent higher than the on shore rate of sexual assault.

I believe that it is certainly possible that the true rate of onboard sexual assault might be higher than what is currently being reported to federal authorities by the cruise industry:

- First, there is no way to reliably assess whether the cruise lines are fully and accurately reporting all onboard sexual assaults to federal authorities. The industry already is expected to report such information, but what's reported is not made public. Thus, it's hard for passengers (or independent third-parties) to confirm whether each incident of sexual assault, including their own, has been fully and properly recorded.
- Second, sexual assault is one of the least reported violent crimes. According to the U.S. Department of Justice, as many as 60% of onshore sexual assault victims decline to report the crime against them. We believe it is likely that many cruise passengers who experience sexual assault on the cruise also will not report the crime (and that such crimes thus will not become part of industry cruise safety statistics). RAINN last week communicated with over 200 rape crisis centers in various states to determine whether any of their clients/hotline callers had been sexually assaulted during a cruise. About 9% of these 200 centers reported being contacted by a cruise victim.
- Third, in today's competitive business climate, cruise lines may have an economic incentive to underreport or misclassify sexual assault crimes. Even if we assume that they are doing their best and would not consciously underreport, cruise personnel may lack the legal knowledge required to properly classify and report sexual crimes to federal authorities. (U.S. college administrators – who also often lack

law enforcement experience -- sometimes encounter similar difficulties in interpreting the federal Clery Act's requirements for reporting on-campus crimes at the nation's college and universities.)

In summary, for those on a cruise, it is easy to forget that the risk of being assaulted onboard a cruise ship is real. It is easy, too, for the vacationing public to forget that, while a cruise ship may resemble a small city in population size, the public on the cruise ship has no law enforcement officials to keep would-be criminals in check or to immediately secure a crime scene and investigate a crime once it occurs.

RECOMMENDATIONS FOR THE 110TH CONGRESS

Impose stricter requirements for reporting onboard incidents of sexual assault (and authorize federal officials to impose penalties for noncompliance with this requirement).

The FBI and the U.S. Coast Guard in 2007 entered into an agreement with the cruise industry, which calls for the industry to voluntarily report certain crimes. This agreement seems to mainly deal with crimes that are voluntarily reported by the industry and might not address crimes that should be, but are not, reported to the FBI. Congress should review this agreement carefully to ensure that the FBI can and will exercise meaningful oversight of cruise industry reporting methods, and to ensure that someone other than the cruise officials has a say in whether or not an incident reported by a passenger meets the threshold for disclosure. If this agreement does not give the FBI the ability to take action against cruise ships (most of which are foreign-flagged vessels) for underreporting or misclassifying sexual crimes, Congress should tighten requirements for the cruise lines. Enhancing the reliability of data on the frequency and nature of crimes on cruises should be the goal.

Provide victims who report sexual assaults during cruises with immediate access (via a telephone or the Web) to rape crisis personnel who are trained to meet the unique needs of Americans traveling overseas, so that cruise victims know they are not alone.

RAINN, the nation's largest anti-sexual assault organization, created and operates the National Sexual Assault Hotline, 800-656-HOPE (in partnership with 1,105 affiliated rape crisis centers, located in every state and the District of Columbia). The Telephone Hotline has helped 1.2 million callers since its inception in 1994. RAINN also recently launched the National Sexual Assault Online Hotline (the nation's first secure, Web-based hotline for rape victims), at www.rainn.org). Finally, RAINN also conducts education and outreach programs to help prevent sexual assault and ensure that perpetrators are brought to justice.

Close to a year ago, RAINN approached one of the largest cruise line companies, Royal Caribbean, to suggest that they establish access from their ships to our Online Hotline and to our 24-hour Telephone Hotline for those instances where a guest or crewmember becomes the victim of a sexual assault while traveling onboard a ship. Our goal is to facilitate both immediate and continuing professional counseling services should a cruise passenger desire and need such services. We are currently engaged in discussions with Royal Caribbean about our proposal to link cruise ship victims with rape crisis hotline personnel while the victims are at sea. We believe that it would be appropriate for the entire industry to provide access to these (or similar hotline) services to any cruise passengers or crew members who are victimized while traveling in international waters.

RAINN also believes that it will be important to equip those hotline personnel who assist cruise victims at sea with certain resources that are uniquely tailored to meet the unique needs of such victims. For example, while the typical (on shore) caller to our Telephone Hotline is seeking information about victim resources in their local community, a caller from a cruise ship at sea typically would need contact information for the consulate or U.S. embassy at the nearest port of call, contact information for the FBI, and information about how to report a sexual assault to cruise line personnel, plus advice on how to seek medical attention and related support services. Cruise victims also may get help from rape crisis centers in their local communities upon their return home.

Of the roughly 200 rape crisis centers, located in various states around the nation, from whom we heard last week, 90% said they do not currently train their personnel to meet the unique needs of victims of cruise ships. Although over half said that they feel fully prepared, and an additional one-third reported that they feel somewhat prepared, to assist cruise victims, 60% said they would find it helpful to receive materials to assist in counseling clients or responding to hotline calls. At least 40% said they would find it helpful to receive contact information for federal agencies that deal with cruise victims; about one-quarter said that they would find it useful to receive a list of international resources that provide assistance to cruise victims; and about one-quarter also said they would appreciate receiving specialized training to help them better meet the unique needs of rape victims on cruises.

Ensure greater oversight of training and conduct of crew members on ships.

The cruise industry needs to take additional steps to ensure that their crewmembers are adequately supervised and that better protocols are instituted and followed to protect victims (crewmembers and passengers alike) in the event that sexual assaults occur on cruises in the future. Royal Caribbean advised us that they recently hired a sexual assault forensic nurse to assist the company in the development of improved evidence collection procedures on their cruises; we encourage the rest of the industry to take similar steps, where appropriate, to ensure that their onboard medical personnel are adequately trained in proper forensic evidence collection methods.

Ensure that cruise lines are accountable to the public to fully report all incidents of sexual assault.

We applaud U.S. Reps. Matsui, Shays, Poe, and Maloney for recently introducing an amendment that would require certain cruise crimes to be publicly disclosed online by the U.S. Coast Guard as well as the cruise industry. This measure recently passed the U.S. House of Representatives as an amendment to a U.S. Coast Guard bill, and we encourage the Senate to pass a similar measure.

Improve the screening and training of crew members who work with passengers.

Many cruise lines serving U.S. passengers employ citizens of a variety of other countries as crewmembers. The screening of crewmembers who work with passengers may not be adequate to fully protect those on cruises against the risks posed by sexual predators. Because crewmembers have been involved in some recent reported sexual assaults, finding a solution to this issue should be a priority for Congress and the industry.

Encourage cruise lines to educate their passengers, before the ship departs, about the onboard risk of sexual assault and what to do if they, or a friend or relative, is assaulted during the voyage.

The cruise industry's advertising materials foster an image of cruise ships as safe and fun havens for vacationing Americans to relax. Parents of children who were assaulted on a cruise occasionally tell us that they let their guard down more while onboard than they would have at home (e.g., by allowing their child to move freely about the ship without adult supervision). Ideally, the entire cruise industry should provide passengers, at the outset of a voyage, with safety information that notes the specific risks to children and youths while traveling on the cruise, gives safety tips for crewmembers and passengers, and explains what to do if you or a friend or family member is assaulted while on a cruise.

CONCLUSION

In closing, thank you for your time and for inviting me to testify. I look forward to continuing to work with you, Mr. Chairman, the Ranking Member, and the other members of this subcommittee on solutions to the important issues discussed at today's hearing.

In: Issues in Cruise Ship Safety and Security ISBN: 978-1-61122-528-0
Editors: Lewis D. Rainer © 2011 Nova Science Publishers, Inc.

Chapter 4

TESTIMONY OF ROSS A. KLEIN, PHD., BEFORE THE SUBCOMMITTEE ON SURFACE TRANSPORTATION AND MERCHANT MARINE INFRASTRUCTURE, SAFETY, AND SECURITY, HEARING ON "CRUISE SHIP SAFETY: EXAMINING POTENTIAL STEPS FOR KEEPING AMERICANS SAFE AT SEA"

A not uncommon problem is the allegation of sexual assault on passengers by crewmembers, particularly cabin, table or bar stewards. Members must have rigorous policies prohibiting socializing between crew and passengers. Any crewmember found in a passenger area where he should not be, should be subject to dismissal for the first offense. A cruise operator must take reasonable care to investigate a crewmember's background before hiring him. There is at present a split of authority between US courts as to whether cruise operators are strictly liable for assaults by crew or whether operators are only liable if they are negligent in hiring or supervising crew members. The majority of the circuits have decided that operators are only liable for negligence. (A Guide to P&I Cover, The Standard, 2007)

The contrast is stark. The cruise industry's insurance carrier states that sexual assault is a not uncommon problem, but the industry itself claims a cruise to be the safest form of commercial transportation. The industry's claim is grand – one which most passengers take at face value.

The Morgans (a pseudonym) took a cruise in 2005, never thinking twice about it being unsafe for their eight-year old middle daughter to go back to the family's cabin on her own. Along the way the youngster became confused and asked a crewmember in uniform for assistance. Instead of helping, the male (wearing a cruise line name plate) allegedly took the girl to a dark end of a corridor where there were no surveillance cameras and he masturbated in front of her. It was subsequently learned that the crewmember had previously worked for a different cruise line that had "do not rehire" marked on his personnel file. But he passed background checks and was hired by the current cruise line. It seems the cruise line also failed to notice that the name under which the man had applied for employment was different than the name on his passport.

Laurie Dishman also believed cruises were safe. She and her best friend in February 2006 chose a cruise to the Mexican Riviera to celebrate thirty years of friendship and to celebrate Laurie's birthday. But things quickly turned from good to bad when a security guard raped Laurie on day two of the cruise. The security guard, she learned later, was actually a janitor "filling in" for security in lounges to check IDs because there were not enough security personnel on board.

The cruise industry would prefer these experiences not be broadcast; when they are made public they are characterized as isolated exceptions or as statistically insignificant. But the fact is that sexual assaults have been recognized as an ongoing problem on cruise ships for decades.

SCOPE OF THE PROBLEM

"Cruise ships are as safe an environment as you can find," was what a Carnival Cruise Lines spokesperson said during a court case involving a fourteen-year-old child who was raped in 1989 on Carnival's *Carnivale*. Rape, he said, "happens in houses, offices, hotels, and parking lots" (Adams 1990: 1).

In this child's case, the rape occurred onboard in a cleaning closet. As the ship was returning to Miami from the Bahamas she went to the family's cabin (while other family members remained on deck) at 5:30 A.M. to check on a suitcase. While in the elevator, a male crewmember – a cleaner onboard the ship – kissed and fondled her. He then dragged her from the elevator to a cleaning closet and raped her on the floor. The girl picked the thirty-two year old crewman, a Colombian national and father of two, out of a line up. In February 1990, he was found guilty of the charges and sentenced to thirty years in prison. The case received considerable attention because it was the first time a crewmember on a foreign-flagged cruise ship had been successfully prosecuted. The assault had occurred while the ship was within U.S. territorial waters (Adams 1990: 1).

Sexual assaults on cruise ships first gained the national media's interest in 1999. One peak was in July 1999 when Carnival Cruise Lines disclosed in the discovery phase of a lawsuit involving an alleged rape that it had received 108 complaints of sexual assaults involving crewmembers in the five year period ending August 1998. Royal Caribbean said it had had fifty-eight reported sexual assaults on its ships during the same five-year period.

Several months earlier an investigative journalist with the *New York Times*, Douglas Frantz, published an article entitled "On Cruise Ships, Silence Shrouds Crimes" where he describes an alarming range of passenger claims of sexual assault and discusses how they were handled by the cruise lines. Based on examination of court records and on interviews with cruise line employees, law enforcement officials, and passengers and their lawyers, Frantz describes

... a pattern of cover-ups that often began as soon as the crime was reported at sea, in international waters where the only police are the ship's security officers. Accused crewmembers are sometimes put ashore at the next port, with airfare to their home country. Industry lawyers are flown to the ship to question the accusers; and aboard ships flowing with liquor, counterclaims of consensual sex are common. The cruise lines aggressively contest lawsuits and insist on secrecy as a condition of settling. (Frantz 1998)

He cites a former chief of security for Carnival Cruise Lines as saying:

You don't notify the FBI. You don't notify anybody. You start giving the victims bribes, upgrading their cabins, giving them champagne and trying to ease them off the ship until the legal department can take over. Even when I knew there was a crime, I was supposed to go in there and do everything in the world to get Carnival to look innocent. (Frantz 1998)

Once a crime is reported, there are problems with preserving evidence. Passenger cabins are routinely cleaned twice a day, so much evidence is destroyed very quickly and there is often a delay between an attack and landing at a U.S. port. Rape experts suggest that cases reported within seventy-two hours provide the best forensic evidence but this time frame is difficult for attacks on a cruise ship. In addition, many victims are likely to delay making a report as long as they are aboard a ship because of fear of reprisal and because there is no independent investigator or rape- treatment centre. Sadly, rapes on cruise ships may often not be reported until it is too late for criminal investigation.

In those cases where a sexual assault is reported in a timely manner, victims and prosecutors were traditionally faced with a common practice among cruise lines to immediately send the accused back home, purportedly because they have violated company policies that prohibit fraternizing between passengers and crew. Reporters for the *Miami New Times* found that in each of five lawsuits against Carnival Cruise Line they reviewed, the employee was swept out of the country immediately after the ship arrived in port. In one case the employee was later rehired by the company and was subsequently served with a summons while at the dock in Los Angeles. Carnival's lawyers successfully argued the Indian citizen couldn't be sued in U.S. courts because American laws did not apply to him: not only is he a foreigner, but the alleged crime took place in Barbados on a ship registered in Panama. The passenger's suit against Carnival Cruise Lines was settled out of court (Korten 2000).

EARLY ATTEMPTS TO ADDRESS THE PROBLEM

Some cruise lines (if not all) undertook initiatives to address the problem of sexual assaults and other crimes, though this was mostly done out of the public's sight. Royal Caribbean, for one, received reports in May/June 1999 from two consultants charged with making recommendations for preventing sexual harassment and assault. The problem was obvious. As one report states, "... improper activity occurs frequently aboard cruise ships, but goes unreported and/or unpunished" (Krohne 1999: 2). The other report acknowledged that "crew members generally understand that if they commit an offence and are caught they are most likely going to lose their job and be returned home, but not spend time in jail" (Greenwood, 1999: 4).

The reports make a range of recommendations, including: increased video surveillance of high risk areas (including the disco bar and dance area, main service corridors on crew decks and key intersections on passenger decks, and youth activity areas); cameras already in place be monitored periodically, at least on a random basis, and be recorded at all times; an increase in the number of security staff by two per ship; and increased training and education of staff and crew members. In addition they recommended that responses to sexual harassment and assault be standardized across brands and ships, that training for medical personnel include an interview protocol for sexual assault incidents, that a staff member be identified and assigned responsibility to serve as an advocate for the target of sexual harassment or assault, that a shore side hotline be established to receive telephone reports of wrongdoing and that investigations be consistent and evenly handled. Given their assumption that cruise passengers were unaware of the prohibition between crew and guest social interactions (and that passengers often, unintentionally, put a crew member in an uncomfortable position by engaging him or her socially), they also recommended better educating passengers and better signage onboard demarcating areas that are "off limits" to passengers. The recommendations are great, but the degree to which they were embraced and implemented is questionable. Many are still being debated and discussed; they are not found in general practice.

The consultants also identified cultural challenges to reducing sexual harassment and assault. For example, senior officers and management need to break from the traditionally hierarchical and militaristic structure of a ship and instead treat their crew and staff members fairly and respectfully. They need to reinforce the need for staff and crew members to treat each other and passengers respectfully. If they wish to prevent sexual harassment and abuse then they must have zero tolerance for both, no matter the rank or position of the offender.

Diverse cultural perceptions of sexual harassment and conduct among a ship's crew present another challenge. There is a diverse population drawn from around the world, and in many of these cultures women, women's rights and sexuality are seen quite differently than they are by most North Americans. These differences need to be addressed through better training and more effective oversight and supervision.

MANAGING PERCEPTIONS

Rather than address the problem head-on, the cruise industry appears to be focused on managing public perceptions. In the midst of the heightened media coverage and interest, four cruise corporations (Carnival Corporation, Royal Caribbean Cruises Limited, Crystal Cruises, and Princess Cruises) representing more than 75 percent of the industry signed a letter of commitment in July 1999. Issued under the auspices of the International Council of Cruise Lines, they pledged a "zero tolerance policy" for crimes committed onboard ships and established an industry standard requiring allegations of onboard crime be reported to the appropriate law enforcement authorities. For vessels calling on U.S. ports, or crime involving U.S. citizens, this meant the Federal Bureau of Investigation (FBI).

Interestingly, cruise lines were already expected to report to the U.S. Coast Guard all crimes involving U.S. citizens on cruise ships but it isn't clear that the information was being reported or sought. U.S. authority in these cases extends from the special maritime and territorial jurisdiction of the United States (USC 18 CFR). Under U.S. Code, the government can exert authority over U.S. territorial seas, any place outside the jurisdiction of a nation with respect to an offence against a U.S. national, and a foreign-flag vessel during a voyage to or from the U.S. where an offence is committed against a U.S. national.

The cruise industry announced its zero tolerance for crime policy with a press release. It reassured passengers of background checks on prospective employees, that crew members violating rules against fraternization with guests would be dismissed, that there were highly trained security personnel on every vessel, and that there were established procedures to investigate, report and refer incidents of onboard crime to appropriate law enforcement authorities. The press release told American passengers that they were protected by U.S. laws, that cruise lines were subject to civil liabilities in U.S. courts, and that they were safer on a cruise ship than in urban or rural America. But it didn't appear to result in greater reporting of crimes.

MINIMIZING THE PROBLEM

The cruise industry has become adept at minimizing the problem. In 1999 it claimed that the number of reported shore side aggravated sexual assaults was at least twenty to fifty times greater than the total number of all reported shipboard assaults of any type. Just seven years later, based on statistics for 2003 through 2005, they testified to a subcommittee of the House of Representatives that the rate of sexual assault on cruise ships was at worst half that found in the US generally (see Fox, 2006). This suggests that there was either as much as a twenty-five-fold increase in sexual assaults between 1999 and 2003 or that the claims made in 1999 were false and unfounded.

The industry's 2006 testimony was questioned a year later through analysis of data presented in a *Los Angeles Times* article (see Yoshino, 2007) which showed the rate of sexual assault was actually almost twice that found in the US (see Klein, 2007). The industry responded privately – they clarified that what they meant in their Congressional testimony was forcible rape, not sexual assaults. They had taken the US rate for forcible rape and labeled them sexual assaults. The integrity of their own data is unclear (e.g., what definitions were used to include/exclude incidents) given that it has not been available for independent analysis and verification.

Most recently, the cruise industry has attempted another method for minimization. Rather than use a standardized rate to reflect incidence of sexual assaults, they now claim "...there is less than a .01 percent chance that a cruise passenger will become the victim of an alleged crime on a cruise vacation" (Dale, 2007) They shifted from a rate based on the daily population on cruise ships (which is consistent with the way rates for crime are computed by the FBI) to a probability based on the total number of cruise ship passengers in a year. Their new representation translates to 10 incidents of crime per 100,000 population. If we use this exact same method to compute the incidence of forcible rape in the state of California (i.e., add together the number of state residents and the number of tourist visitors in a year) it yields a rate of 0.0025 percent, well below the industry's rate of 0.01 percent. But the comparison needs to be treated with caution given that the method by which it is computed is not conventionally accepted as a means for reflecting crime rates.

Shifting definitions is another method used for minimizing the incidence of sexual assaults. As already mentioned, the cruise industry meant "forcible rapes" when they used the label "sexual assaults" in their 2006 testimony before a House of Representatives subcommittee. The difference between the two terms is not trivial. The rate of forcible rape excludes many crimes that fall under the accepted definition for sexual assault, including child sexual abuse and exploitation for sexual purposes, unwanted sexual contact, and unwanted sexual acts. The definition of sexual assault, as it well should be, is broad and includes acts against children, men, and women and which involve unwanted sexual touch, unwanted sexual activity (including but not limited to forcible rape) and sexual exploitation.

Table 1. RCI "Reported Sex Related Incidents" 2003 – 2005
Number of Reported Incidents and Annualized Rate per 100,000 by Ship

Ship	Inappropriate Touch	Sexual Harassment (SH)	Sexual Assault (SA)	SH+SA (annual per/100,000)	Crew-Crew	Guest-Guest	Crew-Guest
Adventure (Double occ: 3114)	0	3	5		0	3	3
Onboard pop=4600 | Incidence/100,000		21.74	36.23	57.97			
Brilliance (Double occ: 2110)	2	6	7		2	2	10
Onboard pop=3100 | Incidence/100,000		64.52	75.27	139.79			
Empress (Double occ: 1600)	2	7	8		2	2	10
Onboard pop=2400 | Incidence/100,000		97.22	111.11	208.33			
Enchantment (Double occ: 1950)	1	4	4		1	2	5
Onboard pop=2900 | Incidence/100,000		45.97	45.97	91.94			
Explorer (Double occ: 3114)	2	13	11		3	3	16
Onboard pop=4600 | Incidence/100,000		94.20	79.71	173.91			
Grandeur (Double occ: 1950)	1	2	3		0	2	3
Onboard pop=2900 | Incidence/100,000		22.99	34.48	57.47			
Jewel (Double occ: 2112)	1	1	0		0	0	2
Onboard pop=3100 | Incidence/100,000		10.75	0.0	10.75			
Legend (Double occ: 1804)	2	2	4		3	2	3
Onboard pop=2700 | Incidence/100,000		24.69	49.38	74.07			
Majesty (Double occ: 2354)	1	10	7		0	2	13
Onboard pop=3500 | Incidence/100,000		95.24	66.67	161.91			
Mariner (Double occ: 3114)	0	6	4	72.47	0	2	6

Table 1. (Continued)

Onboard pop=4600	Incidence/100,000		43.48	28.99			
Monarch (Double occ: 2354)	6	5	15	190.48	2	8	13
Onboard pop=3500	Incidence/100,000		47.62	142.86			
Navigator(Double occ: 3114)	3	6	8	101.45	0	1	13
Onboard pop=4600	Incidence/100,000		43.48	57.97			
Radiance (Double occ: 2110)	4	7	3	107.53	1	2	10
Onboard pop=3100	Incidence/100,000		75.27	32.26			
Rhapsody (Double occ: 2000)	0	3	7	111.10	0	2	5
Onboard pop=3000	Incidence/100,000		33.33	77.77			
Serenade (Double occ: 2112)	0	5	2	75.27	1	3	3
Onboard pop=3100	Incidence/100,000		53.76	21.51			
Sovereign (Double occ: 2276)	1	5	7	114.65	2	1	9
Onboard pop=3400	Incidence/100,000		49.02	65.63			
Splendour (Double occ: 1804)	1	2	0	24.69	0	0	3
Onboard pop=2700	Incidence/100,000		24.69	0.0			
Vision (Double occ: 2000)	7	4	4	88.88	3	2	10
Onboard pop=3000	Incidence/100,000		44.44	44.44			
Voyager (Double occ: 3114)	2	11	14	181.16	3	7	17
Onboard pop=4600	Incidence/100,000		79.71	101.45			
Totals	36	102	113		24	50	151
Onboard pop=64000	Incidence/100,000		53.12	58.85	111.97	10.7%	22.2%	67.1%
US Rate for sexual assaults				32.20			

Place of Incident: Unknown (26.6%), Pax Cabin (20.1%), Bar/Disco (10.8%), Other (6.0%), Dining Area (5.4%), Spa/Salon (5.4%), Public area (4.8%), Cabin - Officer/Crew (3.6%), Corridor (3.0%), Deck area (2.7%), Ashore (2.7%), Child/teen area (2.4%), Elevator (1.8%), Swimming Pool (1.5%), Crew area (1.5%), Public restroom (1.5%)

Explanatory Notes for Table 1

Data in this table was provided as part of discovery in a lawsuit involving the sexual assault of a passenger by a crew member. As such, the data only includes incidents reported to the cruise line and in turn reported in discovery. Given the limited purpose of the discovery request, it is suspected that incidents involving two crew members are under-reported.

The table shows reported incidents that have been labeled by the victim and/or cruise line as inappropriate touch, sexual harassment, sexual assault, or sexual battery. Cases of sexual battery have been included under the label "sexual assault."

The raw data included 41 incidents labeled inappropriate touching, 92 incidents labeled sexual harassment, 114 incidents labeled sexual assault, and 12 incidents labeled sexual battery. After cleaning for accurate labeling, eight incidents were dropped because they were wholly mislabeled; they are not included in the table.

The table shows both the ship's passenger numbers (assuming double occupancy) and an estimate of total ship population that includes crew members and additional passengers given that many ships sail with more passengers than the double occupancy figure.

The comparison of reported incidents of sexual assault with the US rate of sexual assault (as defined by the cruise industry as only forcible rapes) must be interpreted with caution. Technically, such a comparison can be misleading, however the cruise industry chose to make this comparison in testimony provided to Congress by James Fox in March 2006 and on that basis to claim that one is safer on a cruise ship than on land. Perhaps more informative is a comparison of Dr. Fox's assertion that there are 17.6 reported incidents of sexual assault per 100,000 with the data in this chart. This chart shows a rate of sexual assault that is 3.33 times greater than that presented by Dr. Fox to Congress; if we look at sexual assault plus sexual harassment the rate of incidence is 6.36 times greater than reported.

Getting a Grip on the Size of the Problem

There is only one independent set of statistics for the rate of sexual assault on cruise ships. These are based on raw data provided by Royal Caribbean International in discovery in a lawsuit in Florida. The data covers all sex related incidents in a three year period from 2003 through 2005, though based on the wording of the discovery request the data likely under-represents incidents involving two crew members. Table 1 shows that data broken down by ship.

As may be seen in Table 1, the rate of sexual assault on cruise ships, compared to the rate of forcible rape in the US, is not half but almost twice the US rate. This rate is validated by data presented by the FBI in Congressional hearings in September 2007 and summarized in Table 2. The table shows an industry-wide (i.e., members of CLIA) rate of sexual assault of 56.9 per 100,000.

The analysis by ship (Table 1) gives some additional insight into the problem. As can be seen there is a wide variation between ships. Some, such as *Jewel of the Seas*, have relatively few incidents. Others, such as *Monarch of the Seas, Empress of the Seas and Voyager of the Seas*, have many. The obvious question is what can be extrapolated from these differences. That question was posed to several Royal Caribbean staff members. Their responses touched on several issues.

One factor is that incidents vary by cruise length and itinerary. Shorter cruises (three or four days in length) often attract a different type of passenger than cruises lasting a week or more. Those on over-weekend mini-cruise may drink more and take greater part in the nightlife, sometimes to excess. They risk becoming more vulnerable to crewmembers or other passengers. There are also special interest cruises (including partial charters or large affinity groups) that attract passengers who are different than the norm depicted in advertising (e.g., swingers, bikers, hard rockers, etc). While it is difficult to assign the degree of increased risk there is reason to believe that passengers are at greater risk on some cruises than on others simply because of the itinerary, the nature of other cruise passengers or cruise length.

Table 2. Comparison of Crime Rate Aboard Cruise Ships: 2003 – 2005 vs 2007

	2003 – 2005[1]			2007[2]	
	Sexual Assault	Robbery		Sexual Assault[3]	Robbery[4]
Offences reported	149	4	Offences reported (146 days)	69	54
Annual average	49.67	1.33	Annualized rate	172	135
Passenger count, 2003 -05	31,068,000	31,068,000	Pax count, April 1 – Aug 24, 2007	4,379,808	4,379,808
Annual average	10,365,000	10,356,000			
Average pax cruise length (days)	6.9	6.9	Average pa x cruise length[5]	7.0	7.0
Annualized pax exposure			Daily pax exposure	209,991	209,991
Annual average pax count x (6.9/365)	195,771	195,771	Passenger count x (7.0/146)		
Daily crew size[6]	86,035	86,035	Daily crew size[6]	92,284	92,284
Total annualized person exposure	281,806	281,806	Total daily (annualized) person exposure	302,275	302,275
Rate of crime per 100,000	17.6	0.5	Rate of crime per 100,000	56.9	44.7

Notes for Table 2:

[1] Source: Statement on Crime aboard Cruise Ships, James Allan Fox, March 7, 2006, in Congressional hearings. Data was for a period of three full years.

[2] Source: Summary of Subject Matter, Subcommittee on Coast Guard and Maritime Transportation Staff, September 17, 2007, Hearing on Cruise Ship Security Practices and Procedures. Data was for a period of 146 days (April 1 – August 24, 2007): equivalent to 0.4 year.

[3] Sexual Assault includes the categories of "sexual assault" (N = 41) and "sexual contact" (N=28). This is consistent with what is understood to have been done for the 2003-2005 data where it is understood that the categories of "sexual act" and "sexual contact" were both viewed as "sexual assaults."

[4] Robbery includes "theft of items valued over $10,000" (N=13) and "theft of items valued at less than $10,000 (N=41)

[5] Source: CLIA Cruise Industry Overview, Marketing Edition 2006 (latest data available)

[6] The same ratio of passenger-to-crew used in 2003-2005 (0.4349675411) is used here.

A large factor in risk to passengers and to crew is the onboard culture set by management. Some ship captains maintain higher expectations and lower tolerance for misbehavior by crewmembers than others. Others, however, may be less respectful to their crew (acting authoritarian and being unfair in decision-making, such as an officer denying promotions to subordinates involved with female crew members he liked) and create an environment that is less healthy for staff and potentially higher risk for passengers. Some workers cited different management styles as a key factor in the rate of incidence of sexual assault and harassment. Some officers provide better role models than others through their own behavior, both in terms of alcohol consumption and treatment of women crew and passengers. A womanizing Captain, or a Captain who allows senior staff to sexually exploit staff/crew and passengers, sets a tone and gives permission to others to behave the same.

Shipboard culture overlaps with the culture from which crewmembers come. Many locations in the world have different attitudes than those commonly held in North America about women's rights and about the nature of relationships between men and women. Specific cultural views of what constitutes sexual harassment and unwanted attention are a possible risk factor. As Greenwood states, "... it was the subjective opinion stated by many officers and crew members that the cultural inclination toward aggressive sexual behavior, general low regard for the status of women, and the attractiveness and charming personalities of these nationals [(referring to one cultural/ethnic group)] is a risk factor to be considered" (1999: 3–4). The problem is that a crewmember may behave in ways that are acceptable in his or her home culture, but that are inappropriate or abusive in North American culture.

There is no simple solution to the problem, but the by-ship comparison suggests that some ships and ship management are doing things right. There are likely things to be learned by focusing on those ships where sex-related incidents are relatively few and comparing them to those where incidents are many. The differences may provide insight and direction for positive change. But this type of analysis is not being done. While the goal of each cruise line should be consistency across the ships in its brand, it is something that is not being achieved (Krohne 1999).

Michael Eriksen, a lawyer who represents victims of crime on cruise ships has another perspective. He says some forms of crew misconduct derive from the cruise industry's business models and hiring practices.

"Crew members live and work in confined quarters, are away from home for extended periods, and work long hours with little downtime, even during port calls. The crew's alienation from normal home and family activities leaves many vulnerable to social entanglements with passengers." (Eriksen 2006: 48)

Eriksen posits that many if not most crewmembers alleged to have committed sexual offences against passengers aboard cruise ships have been cabin stewards, bartenders, dinner waiters, or others whose jobs involve daily passenger contact. He suggests:

"To deter such misbehavior, a cruise line must do more than write up a 'zero tolerance' policy and pay lip-service to it. Criminals aboard cruise ships, like those elsewhere, commit crimes because they perceive a minimal risk of detection and prosecution. Some cruise lines fail to install sufficient surveillance cameras in public areas to identify and deter potential perpetrators. Other carriers fail to hire enough supervisors and security guards to adequately keep tabs on the rest of the crew. Some carriers fail to make it clear to crewmembers that zero tolerance also applies to crew-passenger contact ashore. Carriers also generally do not warn passengers to be wary of crew member misconduct." (Eriksen 2006:49)

It Isn't Just Sexual Assaults

The first hearings in the House of Representatives in December 2005 were not concerned with sexual assaults. Their initial focus was on a cluster of cases where a passenger disappeared from a cruise ship. The issue was raised in June 2005 in a Business Journal of Jacksonville article written by Mary Moewe. She had found that since 2000 at least twelve cruise ship passengers had gone overboard or disappeared in eleven incidents involving cruise ships that frequent U.S. ports. Two passengers were rescued, two were confirmed dead and eight are still missing. These eight remain a mystery (Moewe 2005).

Unbeknownst to Moewe, the numbers were actually much higher. Because no cruise line or corporation kept track of persons going overboard and no federal agency had responsibility for monitoring these events, she was left to rely on information that was readily available. The most comprehensive list of persons going overboard from cruise ships at the time was online at Cruise Junkie dot Com (see <www.cruisejunkie.com/Overboard.html>). The site reports forty-seven incidents during the same time period covered by

Moewe's article; in nine cases the person was rescued alive. Some cases were clearly suicide, some were accidents and many remained mysterious. Alcohol was a factor in a fair number of suicides and accidents; large gambling losses were a factor in at least three cases and an argument with a spouse or traveling companion preceded four incidents (three men, one woman – in two of these cases the passenger was rescued alive). There was a single case where one passenger was observed throwing another overboard. In September 2001 Myrtha Vogt, a sixty-nine year old woman from New Mexico, was pushed overboard, as her husband watched, by a fellow passenger who was a former mental patient. They were on the third day of an eleven-day cruise of Norway's fjords.

Some of the unexplained disappearances include: Cris Allen Swartzbaugh, a thirty-nine-year-old man who disappeared between Tahiti and Raiatea in the South Pacific the first night of a cruise aboard the *Paul Gauguin* in April 2000; Manuelita Pierce, a thirty-nine-year-old woman who disappeared without a trace at the end of her weeklong Caribbean cruise aboard Royal Caribbean's *Enchantment of the Seas* in October 2000; Randall Gary, a fifty-year-old psychotherapist who in May 2003 disappeared from Holland America Line's *Veendam* somewhere between Vancouver and Alaska; Merrian Carver, a forty-year-old woman who in May 2004 disappeared from an Alaska cruise aboard Celebrity Cruises' *Mercury*; Annette Mizener, a thirty-seven-year-old woman who disappeared from a nine day Mexican Riviera cruise aboard Carnival Pride in December 2004 – in her case the surveillance camera viewing the deck area from where she disappeared, apparently following a struggle, was covered by a map of the ship; and in May 2005 Hue Pham (age seventy- one) and his wife of forty-nine years, Hue Tran (age sixty-seven), disappeared in the Caribbean between the islands of Barbados and Aruba from *Carnival Destiny*. What started out as a Mother's Day gift – a seven night Caribbean cruise with their daughter and granddaughter – turned into a tragic and mysterious disappearance. There were common patterns in these cases: search for the missing passenger was either not undertaken or was inordinately delayed, there appeared to be an absence of investigation, and in some cases law enforcement authorities were not initially notified.

While these cases suggest a problem, the disappearance of George Allen Smith IV, a twenty-six- year-old on his honeymoon aboard the *Brilliance of the Seas* in the Mediterranean in July 2005, immediately captured the world's attention and interest and catapulted passenger disappearances into the public eye. The newlyweds had been drinking heavily and gambling at the ship's casino before his disappearance. The story that emerged was that while

George's wife, Jennifer Hegel- Smith, lay passed out on a floor far from the couple's cabin (and with no recollection of events), George was taken back to his cabin by some drinking buddies who claim they put him to bed. The next morning a youngster in a nearby cabin reported seeing blood on a canopy above a life boat under the Smith cabin and an investigation determined that at least one of the Smiths was missing. Jennifer was located that morning in the gym, unaware that anything had happened.

George's disappearance was reported to local Turkish authorities that came aboard to investigate. To this day, it appears the investigation remains open and conclusions have yet to be drawn. There is some indication that foul play was involved, and some believe they know who was involved, but no one has been formally identified or charged.

In late-June 2006, Jennifer reached a settlement with the cruise line over her husband's disappearance. George's parents the same day filed suit against the cruise line claiming the cruise line deliberately and intentionally portrayed the incident as an accident, and hampered a full- blown, appropriate investigation into the facts and circumstances of George's death. Specifically, they claim the cruise line delayed reporting the incident to the FBI, deciding instead to report the case to Turkish authorities. When Royal Caribbean did contact the FBI, the suit claims the cruise line failed to tell authorities about loud noises and arguing in Smith's cabin and the discovery of blood inside and outside the cabin. As well, the family accuses Royal Caribbean of contaminating a potential crime scene by sending crew members into the cabin to investigate and take photographs and by cleaning blood from the canopy above a lifeboat.

The Smith case dominated news media in the United States for months and was the focus of stories in both print and television magazines. It particularly caught the attention of Smith's member of Congress, Christopher Shays, who was aware of some of the other cases involving disappearances from cruise ships (including the case of Merrian Carver) and who pushed for and who chaired the first two Congressional hearings (December 2005 and March 2006). The latter shifted the spotlight to sexual assaults.

The other issue raised in the March 2006 hearing was robbery and theft. The industry claimed then that there was only four known robberies industry-wide in the three year period, 2003 – 2005. That meant an annual rate of 1.33. As seen in Table 2, the FBI reported in 2007 an annualized rate of 135. That yields a rate of 44.7 per 100,000. This is 100 times greater than what the industry admitted to in its March 2006 testimony.

Getting a Handle on Crime

It is not surprising to most that crimes would occur on cruise ships, much the same as they do on land. However there are features of a cruise vacation – excessive drinking, uninhibited sociality, shipboard culture, and not trivially the industry's mantra that cruise vacations are virtually safe – that raise the risk higher than what would be expected on land and certainly higher than most passengers expect. Like dealing with an alcoholic, the first thing the cruise industry needs to do is to admit that there is a problem. Only then can they begin to address the problem and seek advice from critics and independent and external analysts. Their current method of obfuscation and excluding from discussion those who disagree with them may have worked in past, but the problem has reached proportions that demand meaningful and significant measures.

The industry will argue that the reporting agreement between CLIA and the Coast Guard/FBI is enough for dealing with the problem. However it is not. The industry has been required to report all crimes against Americans for more than a decade (first under USC 18 CFR and later by their zero tolerance pledge in 1999), but they obviously weren't if we compare the incidence before and after April 2007 when the industry's voluntary agreement with the FBI and Coast Guard took effect. The agreement is a positive step, but it has little value when data is collected and then kept secret. There is no regular public reporting of crime on cruise ships. An amendment to HR 2830 offered by Representative Doris Matsui of California (and co-sponsored by Representatives Poe, Maloney and Shays) and passed earlier this year as part of the Coast Guard Reauthorization Bill will change that.

It requires that data collected by the FBI be made available via the Internet, broken down by cruise line, and that the link to the data be clearly displayed on each cruise line's website.

The only apparent weakness of this approach is that it does not define what constitutes a crime. This is important given the industry's propensity for manipulating definitions. It would be helpful to clearly state what actions or behavior is reportable without leaving wiggle room for misinterpretation or under-reporting. Some might argue this approach is based in basic distrust of the cruise industry. The distrust is based in experience. The industry consistently misrepresented and lied about its environmental practices during the 1990s and early 2000s. It has also, intentionally or unintentionally, under-represented the incidence of crimes to Congress and to its customers. It is not necessarily the safest mode of commercial transportation and should not purport to be.

Recommendations

In addition to the need for standardized definitions for reportable crimes, it would also make sense to extend mandatory reporting laws found in virtually every US jurisdiction with regard to child sexual abuse so that they also apply to cruise ships. Why should cruise ships operating out of US ports and carrying American citizens be treated differently than other jurisdictions, especially when it comes to victimization of our youngest citizens? It may also be prudent to have mandatory reporting for all sexual assaults (i.e., sexual contact, sexual acts, forcible rape, and any other incident involving unwanted sexual activity). However, as already stated, clear definitions need to provided so that all crimes be reportable and reported. As well, this data should be public and available to persons thinking about or planning to take a cruise. They need to have information that counterbalances the cruise industry's grand claims about passenger safety.

A second set of recommendations emerges from the 1999 reports by consultants hired by Royal Caribbean Cruises Limited. Many of the recommendations are spot on but have not been implemented or have been implemented in a haphazard and inconsistent manner. Some that still need better implementation include: standardizing the response to incidents of crime across all ships and across brands; independent advocates/counselors onboard who are available to support and care for victims; a hotline reporting system off ship that may be used by those who not surprisingly will feel unsafe about reporting an incident onboard; better surveillance and greater use of CCTV cameras in key areas of the ship, which are regularly monitored and tapes stored for a reasonable period of time (at least as long as the time allotted by the cruise passenger contract for bringing legal action against a carrier) – videos that are not regularly screened give crew members confidence that they are likely to get away with illegal activity; better education of crew and passengers about safety, security, and about the limited nature of permitted interactions between passengers and crew/service staff; and, of key importance, effecting a meaningful and significant change in shipboard culture and tolerance for misdeeds. Many crimes occur because perpetrators know they will not be caught, and if caught they will not be punished.

There is also great room for improvement on a very concrete level. Many recommendations are contained in the International Cruise Victims Association's (ICV) 10-point program. Given that ICV is a grassroots organization comprised largely of people who have experienced crime onboard a cruise ship (or whose family member(s) has/have), and that they speak loudly for themselves, I won't attempt to summarize what they have to say. Their insights are based on direct experience and their recommendations are informed by the pain and suffering they have endured. They can express better than I many of the things the industry could and should be doing that it isn't.

REFERENCES

Adams, Margaret. (1990). *"Rape Case Threatens Cruise Industry Image: Girl, 14, Says Crewman Assaulted Her,"* Miami Herald (Broward Edition), February 5.

Dale, Terry. (2007). *Letter from CLIA to the Chair of the House Subcommittee on Coast Guard and Marine Transportation*, December 19, 2007.

Eriksen, Michael. (2006). *"Love Boats on Troubled Waters,"* Trial 43, 3 (March).

Fox, James Alan. (2006). *"Statement on Crime Aboard Cruise Ships,"* Testimony Before the Committee on Government Reform, United States House of Representatives, Subcommittee on National Security, Emerging Threats and International Relations, March 7.

Frantz, Douglas. (1998). *"On Cruise Ships, Silence Shrouds Crimes,"* New York Times, November 16. Available at <www.nytimes.com/ library/ national/ 111698cruise-ship-crime.html> (Accessed July 14, 1999)

Greenwood, Don. (1999). *"Reducing Sexual Assaults on Cruise Ships: Risk Assessment and Recommendations,"* Unpublished consultant's report. June 7.

Klein, Ross A. (2007). *"Crime Against Americans on Cruise Ships,"* Testimony Before the Committee on Transportation and Infrastructure, United States House of Representatives, Subcommittee on Coast Guard and Maritime Transportation, March 27. Available at <transportation percent2 0Guard/200 7032 7/Klein.pdf>

Korten, Tristram. (2000). *"Carnival? Try Criminal: What happens when a female passenger is assaulted on a cruise ship? Not much."* Miami New

Times, February 3-9. Available at <www.miaminewtimes. com/2000-02-0 3/news/carnival-try-criminal> (Accessed February 5, 2000)

Krohne, Kay. (1999). Unpublished consultant's report examining current efforts of Royal Caribbean Cruises Ltd. in the area of preventing sexual harassment and assault. May 26.

Moewe, M. C. (2005). *"Disappearances Leave Mystery,"* Business Journal of Jacksonville, June 3. Available at *<www.bizjournals.com/ jacksonvill /stories/2005/06/06/story1.html>* (Accessed July 4, 2005)

Yoshino, Kimi. (2007). *"Cruise Industry's Dark Waters: What Happens at Sea Stays There as Crimes on Lineres Go Unresolved,"* Los Angeles Times, January 20. Available at <www.latimes.com/business/la-fi-cruise20jan20, 1,648572   7.story?   track=   crosspromo   &coll=la-   headlines-business&ctrack= 1&cset=true> (Accessed January 20, 2007)

In: Issues in Cruise Ship Safety and Security   ISBN: 978-1-61122-528-0
Editors: Lewis D. Rainer   © 2011 Nova Science Publishers, Inc.

Chapter 5

HEARING ON "CRUISE SHIP SECURITY PRACTICES AND PROCEDURES"

Subcommittee on Coast Guard and Maritime Transportation Staff

SUMMARY OF SUBJECT MATTER

TO: Members of the Subcommittee on Coast Guard and Maritime Transportation
FROM: Subcommittee on Coast Guard and Maritime Transportation Staff
SUBJECT: Hearing on Cruise Ship Security Practices and Procedures

PURPOSE OF HEARING

On September 19, 2007, at 11:00 a.m. in 2165 Rayburn House Office Building, the Subcommittee will meet to hold a hearing on cruise ship security practices and procedures. During a Subcommittee hearing in March 2007, entitled "Crimes Against Americans on Cruise Ships," representatives of the Cruise Lines International Association, Inc. ("CLIA") and the victims and family members of victims of alleged crimes on cruise ships agreed at the Chairman's request to meet to discuss: (1) potential refinements in procedures for reporting alleged crimes on cruise ships to U.S. authorities; and (2) specific measures that could be implemented to improve the safety and security of passengers on cruise ships. These parties further agreed to re-appear before the Subcommittee to provide an update on the status of their discussions. This hearing is intended to receive that update and to examine whether the security practices and procedures aboard cruise ships are adequate to ensure the safety of all passengers.

BACKGROUND

Reporting of Crimes on Cruise Ships

There are approximately 200 ocean-going cruise ships in operation worldwide. Each ship carries an average of 2,000 passengers and 950 crew members. It is estimated that 10.6 million Americans will take a cruise from a U.S. port in 2007.

- With the exception of two cruise ships operating in the coastwise trade in Hawaii, all of the cruise ships that call on U.S. ports are registered in foreign countries. As such, these foreign-flagged vessels are subject to the laws of the countries in which they are registered and to applicable provisions from international treaties that address the safety of passenger vessels (predominantly the International Convention on Safety of Life at Sea ["SOLAS"]). Non-U.S.-flagged ships are not subject to U.S. laws that apply to U.S.-flagged vessels or land-based U.S. corporations. They are subject to U.S. laws only when they operate in U.S. territorial waters (which extend 12 miles from the U.S. coastline) or as specific conditions are imposed on such vessels as a pre-requisite to their entry into a U.S. port.

Cruise ships with foreign registries are required by law to report alleged crimes occurring on board their vessels to U.S. authorities when they occur within U.S. territorial waters (per Title 33 of the Code of Federal Regulations, section 120.220). Under current law, cruise ships are not required to report crimes to U.S. authorities that occur outside U.S. territorial waters under any circumstances (even if U.S. nationals are involved). However, the Coast Guard is currently reviewing U.S. regulations regarding the reporting of crimes to U.S. authorities occurring outside U.S. territorial waters — and reports that it is considering requiring such crimes to be reported to U.S. authorities for vessels on cruise ships that enter or depart a U.S. port.

However, Title 18 of the U.S. Code identifies specific crimes over which the United States may assert criminal jurisdiction under what is known *as* the Special Maritime and Territorial Jurisdiction. Such jurisdiction applies if:

1. The ship on which the crime occurs — even if is not registered in the United States — is owned in whole or in part by U.S. entities and the ship is in the admiralty and maritime jurisdiction of the United States and out of the jurisdiction of any particular state;

2. The alleged offense is committed by or against a U.S. national and is committed outside the jurisdiction of any nation;

3. The crime occurs in U.S. territorial waters, regardless of the registration of the vessel or the nationality of the victim or perpetrator; or

4. The victim or perpetrator is a U.S. national on board a vessel during a voyage that departed from or will arrive in a U.S. port.

If committed under any of the circumstances described above, the crimes over which the U.S. may assert jurisdiction include arson, assault, maiming, embezzlement or theft, receipt of stolen property, murder, manslaughter, attempt to commit murder or manslaughter, kidnapping, malicious mischief, robbery and burglary, stowing away, aggravated sexual abuse, sexual abuse, abusive contact of a minor or ward, abusive sexual contact, terrorism, and transportation for illegal sexual activity.

On April 1, 2007, CLIA, the Federal Bureau of Investigation ("FBI"), and the United States Coast Guard implemented a voluntary agreement that sought to define the processes that will govern the reporting by cruise lines to the FBI and the Coast Guard of crimes over which the U.S. Special Maritime and Territorial Jurisdiction may apply.

Under the procedures laid out in the agreement, CLIA members have committed to contact by telephone the nearest FBI Field Office or Legat (a legat is an FBI legal attaché office maintained in a U.S. embassy or consulate) as soon as possible to report any incidents involving the alleged serious violation of a U.S. law, including homicide, suspicious deaths, missing U.S. Nationals, kidnapping, assault with serious bodily injury, sexual assaults as defined in title 18 of the United States Code, tampering with vessels, and theft of items valued at greater than $10,000. Following the establishment of telephonic contact, CLIA members have committed to follow-up their oral reports with standardized written reports.

CLIA members have further committed to submit reports to the United States Coast Guard National Command Center via either facsimile or e-mail. The Coast Guard in turn has committed to forward these reports to appropriate federal investigative agencies (when the appropriate agency is not the FBI). The FBI is identified as the U.S. agency responsible for deciding whether to investigate or respond to alleged crimes. The Coast Guard does respond to reports of people overboard or other serious incidents with appropriate immediate intervention, including search and rescue operations.

For incidents that do not fall into any of the categories enumerated in the voluntary agreement (such as the theft of items valued at less than $10,000), the agreement specifies that cruise lines may email or fax notification to the local FBI Field Office or Legat. The agreement further states that criminal activity not meeting the reporting criteria enumerated in the voluntary agreement can be reported to the proper state or local law enforcement authorities. Further, narcotics activities are to be reported as per agreements in place with the Drug Enforcement Administration, Immigration and Customs Enforcement, and Customs and Border Protection.

Upon receipt of reports of alleged serious violations of U.S. law, the agreement states that the FBI will determine on a case by case basis whether the reported information will be investigated, and whether the investigation will be conducted by a Field Office or Legat. When the case is referred to a Legat, the Legat's legal authority to conduct the investigation and/or to secure the approval of foreign authorities to conduct investigations will be determined on a case by case basis. Legats will coordinate all aspects of any investigation that they undertake, including crime scene preservation, evidence collection, and interviews of victims and witnesses. Legats will also determine whether investigations will be conducted in the Legat's territory or when a vessel reaches its next port of call. The agreement specifies that each cruise line will make available all accommodations necessary to support an FBI investigation.

Since the agreement was put in place, the Coast Guard reports that 4,379,808 passengers have embarked on cruises operated by cruise lines that are members of CLIA. This figure includes all passengers of all nationalities embarking from all ports; it is not limited to passengers that have embarked from U.S. ports or to passengers that are U.S. citizens.

The FBI reports that 207 incidents have been reported by CLIA member cruise lines to the Bureau from April 1, 2007 through August 24, 2007 — meaning that reported incidents have involved fewer than .01 percent of passengers on cruise ships during that period. These incidents are presented by type in Table 1 below.

Among the types of incidents identified as "other," the FBI has provided the breakdown of the types of incidents as shown in Table 2 below.

From the 207 incidents reported by the FBI, the Bureau has opened 18 case files, including case files for 13 alleged sexual assaults, three missing persons, and two alleged physical assaults. The FBI further reports that they have made one arrest as a result of an investigation of an alleged sexual assault.

Table 1. Total Incidents Reported by CLIA Members to the FBI (From April 1, 2007 through August 24, 2007)

Type of Incident	Number of Reports
Death — homicide	0
Death — suspicious	0
Missing U.S. national	4
Kidnapping	0
Assault with serious bodily injury	13
Sexual assault	41
Tampering with vessels	1
Theft of items valued over $10,000	13
Other	135
Total	207

Table 2. Breakdown of Incidents Reported to the FBI and Classified as "Other" (From April 1, 2007 through August 24, 2007)

Type of Incident	Number of Reports
Other - Theft of items valued at less than $10,000	41
Other — simple assault	36
Other — sexual contact	28
Other — death (including two suicides, one death from natural causes and one accidental death)	4
Other — no re-board	4
Other — miscellaneous	22
Total	135

Meetings between CLIA and Cruise Incident Victims

Since the Subcommittee convened a hearing on cruise ship crime in March 2007, CLIA and the victims and families of victims of incidents — including alleged crimes — on cruise ships have held several different meetings to assess ways of improving security and safety for passengers on cruise ships.

Representatives of CLIA met with representatives of the International Cruise Victims Organization (ICV) on July 26, 2007, in Washington, D.C., to discuss the 10-point plan developed by ICV. This meeting was convened following an initial meeting between the president of CLIA and the president of the ICV in May 2007 to lay the groundwork for discussions of cruise ship safety between the two organizations.

Representatives of CLIA and a number of CLIA member cruise lines met a wide group of victims and families of victims of alleged crimes on cruise ships (including both members and nonmembers of the ICV) on August 13 and 14, 2007, in Miami, Florida, to discuss proposals for improving safety on cruise ships.

Further, representatives of CLIA also met representatives of the FBI on July 25, 2007 in Washington, D.C., to discuss the voluntary agreement among the FBI, the Coast Guard, and CLIA; and the role of the FBI in responding to alleged crimes committed on cruise ships.

Issues to be Considered During the Hearing

The Subcommittee will receive testimony from the FBI, the Coast Guard, and CLIA regarding the implementation of the voluntary incident reporting agreement, including assessing the level of compliance among cruise lines with this agreement as well as assessing whether the FBI is receiving the information it needs in a timely manner to protect Americans.

The Subcommittee will also receive testimony from CLIA and from victims and family members of victims of incidents on cruise ships to assess the status of discussions between the parties regarding specific measures that they believe should be implemented to improve cruise ship safety.

PREVIOUS COMMITTEE ACTION

The Subcommittee on Coast Guard and Maritime Transportation previously held a hearing entitled "Crimes Against Americans on Cruise Ships" on March 27, 2007.

In: Issues in Cruise Ship Safety and Security   ISBN: 978-1-61122-528-0
Editors: Lewis D. Rainer   © 2011 Nova Science Publishers, Inc.

Chapter 6

STATEMENT OF REAR ADMIRAL WAYNE JUSTICE, ASSISTANT COMMANDANT FOR RESPONSE, U.S. COAST GUARD, DEPT. OF HOMELAND SECURITY, BEFORE THE SUBCOMMITTEE ON COAST GUARD & MARITIME TRANSPORTATION, HEARING ON "CRUISE SHIP CRIME: PRACTICES AND PROCEDURES"

Good morning Mr. Chairman and distinguished members of the Subcommittee. I am honored to appear before you to provide an update on the Coast Guard's role and actions taken to assess and address concerns about crime on cruise ships. I will focus my brief remarks on our progress since March to both clarify and highlight the scope of mandatory cruise ship crime reporting requirements, and to implement more expansive voluntary reporting of crimes on cruise ships.

The Coast Guard is committed to improving the overall safety and security of the maritime transportation system. The cruise ship industry is a very important sector within this system. Each year, cruise ships around the world carry over eight million U.S. citizens as passengers. As I reported in March, nearly all cruise ships are foreign-flagged and subject to the exclusive jurisdiction of their flag State when operating seaward of any other State's territorial sea. Much of the alleged crime involving cruise ships is clearly under the jurisdiction of either a foreign coastal State or the cruise ship's Flag State, and therefore may not be within the jurisdiction of the United States. Determining whether the United States may have authority, jurisdiction, and resources to intervene in cases involving United States citizens aboard foreign-flagged vessels beyond the U.S. territorial sea is situationally-dependent, varying with timing and content of initial reporting.

The primary role of the Coast Guard with respect to cruise ship crimes is establishing and facilitating Federal reporting requirements and procedures in a manner consistent with domestic and international law. These procedures enable notification to and decision-making by appropriate investigative agencies. By establishing maritime crime reporting requirements and facilitating delivery of incident reports through the Coast Guard's network of maritime command and operations centers, the Coast Guard supports the Federal Bureau of Investigation (FBI) in its lead investigative and statistical analysis roles. To further develop the interagency role, the Coast Guard led a successful effort this year to ensure national-level agency and industry alignment regarding the application of current Federal regulations.

Current Federal regulations (33 CFR 120.100 and 120.220) establish reporting requirements for all passenger vessels over 100 gross tons, carrying more than 12 passengers for hire, making voyages lasting more than 24 hours, any part of which is on the high seas, and for which passengers are embarked or disembarked in the United States or its territories. The owner, operator, charterer, or vessel security officer of a covered vessel must report each breach of security, unlawful act, or threat of an unlawful act against any covered vessel, or against any person aboard it, that occurs in a place subject to the jurisdiction of the United States Government.

The Coast Guard and the FBI, in consultation and coordination with the Departments of State and Justice, interpret the current regulations as applying to acts committed in U.S. inland waters and the U.S. territorial sea. To the extent permitted by international law, regulations also apply aboard any foreign vessel seaward of U.S. territorial waters during a voyage having a scheduled departure from or arrival in the United States with respect to an offense committed by or against a national of the United States. For example, an offense committed against a U.S. national on the high seas or in foreign territorial waters aboard a foreign-flagged cruise ship that embarked from or intended to call on a U.S. port would be subject to the reporting requirement as a de facto condition of port entry.

Covered incidents must be reported to both the Coast Guard and to the local office of the FBI. The Coast Guard's National Command Center in

Washington, DC immediately distributes all reports received to the FBI and the appropriate Coast Guard Captain of the Port. Where a foreign state has concurrent jurisdiction with the United States, that is, a crime takes place in the foreign state's territorial waters or on board a vessel in international waters flagged in a foreign State, the cruise line or cruise vessel should notify the appropriate authorities of the foreign state, at least simultaneously with notification to U.S. authorities. We have communicated our interpretation of the scope of the current mandatory reporting requirements to the Cruise Line International Association (CLIA) and reiterate them here today as part of my public statement for the record.

Our current regulatory approach with respect to mandatory incident reporting is consistent with well-settled principles of international law regarding the extraterritorial application of a coastal State's domestic laws. However, the mandatory requirements to report incidents under the current regulations do not effect and may not always be coextensive with the extraterritorial criminal investigative and arrest authorities of U.S. law enforcement agencies. This is because the basis of our legal authority, under both international and domestic law, to compel foreign flag vessels not calling on the United States to report crimes committed by or against U.S. citizens seaward of our territorial jurisdiction is different from the authority employed by the United States to investigate and potentially prosecute such crimes.

In order to facilitate increased reporting, the Coast Guard worked closely with the FBI and the Cruise Line International Association (CLIA) throughout 2006 and early 2007 to reinforce the scope of the mandatory reporting requirements, and to develop voluntary reporting procedures for serious offenses committed by or against U.S. citizens aboard cruise ships that are beyond the scope of the mandatory reporting requirements. This effort represented the first disciplined effort to gather serious crime statistics with respect to cruise ships frequented by U.S. citizens regardless of whether such vessels call in the United States. Given the legal and operational environment that I described when I testified in March, we viewed this voluntary reporting system as the most promising and viable option in the near term for improving and expanding cruise ship crime reporting and investigative response.

As expected, many in the cruise industry reinforced compliance with existing mandatory reporting requirements and embraced the opportunity to report and improve responses to serious crimes affecting U.S. citizens. Collectively, the Coast Guard and the FBI received and processed 207 incident reports in the first six months of the program. The vessels making those 207 reports carried over 4,379,000 passengers during the period. As I mentioned earlier, it is the Coast Guard's role to establish reporting requirements and the FBI's role to determine the appropriate Federal investigative response in specific cases and compile crime statistics for policy analysis. Accordingly, I will defer to the FBI to provide more detailed investigative and analytical context for the reporting. From the Coast Guard's overall maritime security perspective, we have no evidence or data to suggest there is significantly more crime or change to the nature of crime affecting U.S. citizens aboard cruise ships.

Based on consultations with FBI, the Coast Guard believes clarifying the scope of the mandatory cruise ship reporting requirements and implementing additional voluntary reporting procedures are working well, contributing to improved situational awareness through transparency, and helping to better inform both the discussion and response with respect to allegations regarding crime on cruise ships. We see no emerging requirement for legislative change regarding incident reporting requirements. We continue to recommend prospective cruise ship passengers assess the level of security and safety on foreign-flagged cruise ships on which they may embark just like they would evaluate their safety and security risks when visiting a foreign country. Congressional hearings like these help highlight that responsibility, and encourage the cruise ship industry to embrace transparency in reporting and crime prevention strategies to remain successful.

It is clear that some serious acts affecting U.S. citizens aboard foreign-flagged cruise ships have brought great sadness to the families of victims. The Coast Guard mourns the losses these families have suffered and we are committed to improving the overall safety and security environment within the maritime domain. The Coast Guard will continue to work with the FBI and the Departments of State and Justice to ensure effective implementation of both mandatory and voluntary reporting procedures, and to intervene at sea when appropriate. Together, the mandatory reporting regulations and the voluntary reporting requirements contribute to improving the safety and security of U.S. citizens aboard cruise ships by leveraging partnerships with industry and improving transparency for consumers.

Thank you for the opportunity to testify today. I look forward to your questions.

In: Issues in Cruise Ship Safety and Security   ISBN: 978-1-61122-528-0
Editors: Lewis D. Rainer   © 2011 Nova Science Publishers, Inc.

Chapter 7

STATEMENT OF SALVADOR HERNANDEZ, DEPUTY ASSISTANT DIRECTOR, FEDERAL BUREAU OF INVESTIGATION, BEFORE THE SUBCOMMITTEE ON COAST GUARD AND MARITIME TRANSPORTATION

Good morning Chairman Cummings, Ranking Member LaTourette, and Members of the -Subcommittee. I appreciate the opportunity to be here today to provide an update on the FBI's work with the U.S. Coast Guard, the cruise line industry and the victims of cruise line crime regarding crime aboard cruise ships.

REPORTING AGREEMENT

I testified earlier this year that, after many months in development, in March 2007, the FBI, the U.S. Coast Guard and the Cruise Lines International Association (CLIA) reached an agreement on voluntary, standardized protocols for CLIA member lines to report allegations of serious violations of U.S. law committed aboard cruise ships. These reporting procedures are in addition to, but not in lieu of, the mandatory reporting requirements, e.g., the requirements of 46 Code of Federal Regulations (CFR) Part 4, or the requirements of 33 CFR Part 120. Further, this reporting does not replace or override any agency responsibilities and coordination mandated by the Maritime Operational Threat Response Plan.

INCIDENT STATISTICS

Pursuant to the agreement, on April 1, 2007, the FBI began collecting and tracking the incident reports submitted by CLIA member lines. I would like to take a few minutes this morning to report on the results of this effort. Through August 24,2007, the FBI received 207 reports from CLIA members. Many of these matters did not require criminal investigation and as such, should be viewed as "incident reports" not "crime reports." For example, reports were received of attempted suicides of passengers, as well as matters with purely civil implications.

Sixteen, or 8%, of all reports involved incidents that occurred while a passenger was ashore outside of the United States and, therefore, outside the jurisdiction of the FBI and other U.S. law enforcement. For example, a passenger . reported that he was robbed by two subjects in a vehicle while ashore in the Bahamas. In matters such as these, the reporting agreement holds that, although cruise lines may report incidents which occurred outside of the United States' jurisdiction to the FBI, they are not required to do so.

Of the 207 incident reports received by the FBI, 39 incidents, or 19%,were responded to and/or investigated by law enforcement other than the FBI. These law enforcement agencies included local police departments in the United States, as well as foreign law enforcement agencies. Nineteen reported incidents occurred while the ship was docked. In the United States, the jurisdiction over an event that occurs aboard a vessel generally lie with the state in whose waters the vessels are moored. Accordingly, a report of a theft of items estimated at $30,000 which was stolen while a ship was docked in Galveston, Texas, was investigated by the Galveston Police Department.

In further breakdown of the incidents that were reported to the FBI during this initial reporting period I provide the following: The agreement with CLIA and the U.S. Coast Guard lists eight categories of incidents which are to be telephonically reported by CLIA members to the nearest FBI field office or Legal Attache office. These matters -- homicide, suspicious death, missing U.s. National, kidnapping, assault with serious bodily injury, sexual assault, firing or tampering with vessels, and theft greater than $10,000 --involve potentially serious violations of U.S. law and are to be called in to theFBI as soon as possible following the incident. After telephonic contact, CLIA members are instructed to follow-up with a standardized written report. All other, less serious matters are reported under a general "other" category and are brought to the FBI's attention by submission of a written report.

During the first five months of reporting under the agreement, there were no reports of homicide, suspicious death or kidnapping aboard CLIA member ships. There were four reports of missing U.s. Nationals. Of these four reports, one involved a husband and wife who took most of their belongings with them and chose not to re-board after docking at a foreign port. The three remaining reports involved passengers whose past histories and behavior while on board the ship strongly suggested they had taken their own lives.

CLIA members reported 13 assaults with serious bodily injury. The FBI opened two investigative cases from these reports, both of which are ongoing. Several matters submitted in the "assault with serious bodily injury" category were, in fact, of lesser seriousness.

The FBI investigates sexual assaults as defined in Title 18 of the United States Code (USC), Sections 2241through 2243 and 2244 (a) and (c). Since April 1, the cruise lines have reported 41 instances of sexual assault. Of these 41 incidents, 19represented allegations of sexual activity generally categorized as rape, three of which occurred on shore, and, thus, outside the jurisdiction of the FBI. Based on the 41 reports, the FBI opened 13 investigative cases. Five of these cases have been closed for reasons of victim reluctance to pursue prosecution or prosecutive declination from the United States Attorney's Office. Eight investigations are ongoing.

During this period, there were 13 reported incidents of theft of more than $10,000. Nine of these incidents involvedjewelry, two involved cash, one involved miscellaneous items from onboard shops, and one involved food products.

There was one report of firing or tampering with vessels.

The remaining 135 incident reports, or 65% of all reports, involved less serious matters such as simple assault, low-dollar loss theft, fraud, suspicious activity, bomb threats, sexual contact, or activity that was not criminal in nature. Sexual contact, defined in 18USC 2244 (b) as, essentially, uninvited touching of a sexual nature, made up 28 reports. Thirty-six of the 135reports involved simple assault matters to include punching, slapping or pushing actions, and 41 reports related to theft of less than $10,000.

Incidents on board ships when investigated by the FBI are documented through investigative files under the "Crimes on the High Seas" classification. Of the 207 incident reports, the FBI opened 18 investigative files. This number is consistent with the number of "Crimes on the High Seas" cases opened annually for the past five years.

Based on my personal involvement in the matter of cruise ship crime reporting over the past year, and the fact that many reports we have received during the first five months of reporting fall outside FBI jurisdiction, do not constitute crimes under U.S. law, or are less serious than characterized by the cruise lines, it is my belief that CLIA member cruise lines are generally making a good faith effort to report all crimes, or allegations of crime, set out under the agreement.

COORDINATION WITH CLIA AND THE INTERNATIONAL CRUISE VICTMS' ASSOCIATION

I would like to briefly update the Subcommittee on other matters which the FBI has undertaken in support of its role in investigating crimes aboard cruise ships. Since I last testified, the FBI has met again with members of the International Cruise Victims' Association. Kendall Carver, whom you will hear from later today, came to FBI Headquarters in July accompanied by two members of his group. I met personally with Mr.Carver and his associates to hear their concerns and to explain the work being done by the Coast Guard, CLIA and the FBI regarding cruise ship crime reporting. Over the past six months, my associates at the FBI and I have met or spoken with CLIA and the Coast Guard regularly to check progress on our reporting protocols to refine those protocols where necessary.

Training

Finally, a note about proactive steps being taken by the FBI and CLIA. When I last testified, I described the training provided by the FBI's Regional Evidence Response Teams (ERT) to cruise line Staff Captains and Security Managers over the last three years. The FBI's ERT Unit in Quantico, Virginia, has recently completed a universal PowerPoint presentation for evidence preservation. This training will be made available to the cruise line industry in the near future.

In closing, the FBI is committed to continuing its work with the cruise'line industry, the U.S. Coast Guard and victims' groups to ensure full reporting of crimes aboard cruise ships and to facilitate more effective first response to such crimes. Thank you Chairman Cummings and members of the Subcommittee for the opportunity to testify today. I am happy to answer any questions you may have.

In: Issues in Cruise Ship Safety and Security   ISBN: 978-1-61122-528-0
Editors: Lewis D. Rainer   © 2011 Nova Science Publishers, Inc.

Chapter 8

TESTIMONY OF LYNNETTE HUDSON, BEFORE THE SUBCOMMITTEE ON COAST GUARD AND MARITIME TRANSPORTATION, HEARING ON "CRUISE SHIP SECURITY PRACTICES AND PROCEDURES"

Hello, I would like to start by thanking Chairman Cummings and the entire Subcommittee for inviting me to testify today concerning Cruise Ship Security Practices and Procedures. I would also like to take this opportunity to personally thank my Congressman, Mike Castle, for his continual support of legislation to protect Americans on cruise ships. Today, I have been provided with a unique opportunity to share my experiences surrounding the death of my father on board a cruise ship. I hope that my testimony will bring to light the necessity of viable safety practices and procedures to eliminate or at least minimize death, injuries and crimes at sea. I am here today on behalf of my father, Richard Liffridge, who died on March 23, 2006 while taking what he believed to be a safe and enjoyable vacation on the Star Princess. In addition, I am also representing the International Cruise Victims Association (ICV), which is an organization formed by grieving family members and victims who have unfortunately experienced preventable tragedies while on cruise ships.

Before I explain the events of that fateful day in March 2006, that changed my life forever, I would be remise if I did not tell you about my father. Richard Liffridge was a devoted husband, father, grandfather and great-grandfather. After 20 years of honorable military service, he retired from the United States Air Force. His Air Force career allowed him to travel to places he might not have otherwise seen such as France, Germany and England. He proudly served his country in the Vietnam and Korean wars. After retiring from the Air Force, my father ironically worked for the Federal Emergency Management Agency (FEMA) for a number years. He subsequently retired and relocated to Locust Grove, GA, to realize his life long dream of retiring in a stable environment while enjoying the company of his family and friends. My father was a dedicated and committed member of the Masons. The Masons are the oldest and largest world wide fraternity dedicated to the brotherhood of man.

On March 19, 2006, my father, his wife, Victoria, and two other couples boarded the Star Princess at Fort Lauderdale, Florida. The three couples planned the seven day cruise to celebrate their collective birthdays. My father had just turned 72 years old eight days prior to their departure. This was his first cruise and he anticipated relaxing and enjoying the company of his wife and close friends. However, during the early morning hours on March 23, 2006, a fire erupted on the eleventh floor deck area of the cruise ship, which then quickly spread to the upper decks severely damaging approximately 79 cabins. This rapidly moving fire produced a black thick smoke, which was later determined to be the by product of combustible materials used in the partitions and balconies. It took an unconscionable hour and a half to extinguish this on board fire which was later determined to have started as a result of a smoldering cigarette discarded on the balcony of a stateroom.

It was difficult to piece together the actual events specifically as they relate to my father on that terrible morning. The information that was relayed to our family was that my father and Victoria were awakened by faint sounds of an alarm and static over the intercom. Victoria got up to determine the cause of the commotion. Upon opening the room door, she noticed a crew member knocking on a door across the hall. The crew member did not say anything to her. Victoria then heard one of her traveling companions yelling, "the ship is on fire, the ship is on fire; everyone get out!" Victoria relayed this information to my father and they proceeded to evacuate. While evacuating, they thoughtfully grabbed wet towels to be used as an aid to them in safely escaping the fire. Meanwhile, the thick black toxic smoke began to fill the corridors and seep under the doorway of their cabin.

Once they opened their cabin door, they were unable to see due to dark smoke filled hallway. To escape, they proceeded to crawl on their hands and knees with the wet towels around their faces for protection. Remembering that there was an emergency exit located close to their cabin, they began crawling in that direction. My father was leading the way with Victoria holding on to his T- shirt. They were able to reach the emergency exit door, but could see flames coming from the other side of the door. The corridor continued to fill with smoke and their visibility was zero. Emergency lighting was not visible nor were there any emergency response teams there to assist them.

As the two tried to crawl towards another escape route, the ship shifted which caused Victoria to be thrown to the opposite side of the corridor. Victoria attempted to make her way back to my father but could not locate him. She was unable to call out his name as the smoke began to fill in her lungs. As she tried to reach out for my father, she heard him say, "Vicky, don't let me die." Unfortunately, she was unable to express reassurance to her husband (my father), but she frantically continued to try to locate him in the dark. Despite her tenacious effort, Victoria wasn't able to locate by father. She began to go in and out of consciousness. Thankfully, there were other passengers to assist her in exiting this chaotic area. It was unclear at that time if my father had made it out of the corridor safely. However, as it would soon be painfully discovered, my father was not successful in escaping this enormous on board fire. My father's lifeless body was found inside the corridor on deck 12 outside a stateroom.

Victoria was taken to a muster station where she sat shivering and unattended for an extended period of time. Victoria was told at that time that all passengers were accounted for. When she specifically asked about my father, she was told he was in another muster station.

Approximately nine hours after the start of the fire, I received a heartbreaking phone call from my brother, Phil. He was calling to tell me that there had been a fire onboard the ship and Dad did not make it. Phil had been contact by Victoria, who was being treated for smoke inhalation at a local Jamaican hospital. How could this be? My father was on a luxury cruise with his wife and friends. I felt like my life came crashing to an end. I fainted after hearing the news. When I came to, I was surrounded by my co-workers. After telling them what happened, some of them were already aware of the ship's fire. Someone printed a CNN story that said cruise line officials reported my father's cause of death as a "heart attack." That same article provided a toll free phone number for family members of passengers to contact for more information.

I called the toll free number several times, but the cruise line representatives told me that they were not able to release any information to me. I felt frantic. It was not until I became irate that the representative attempt to assist me. I learned at that time that Princess Cruises had my contact information on file. I was provided with the phone number for the local hospital where Victoria was being treated. After speaking with Victoria, she asked if Princess Cruise line ever contacted me as I was listed as my father's emergency contact person.

In an effort to accommodate the surviving passengers, Princess Cruise line offered a full refund and 25% discount on a future cruise. They also paid to transport travelers home and for lodging during that transition. It is clear that Princess Cruise line made a genuine effort to accommodate those surviving passengers that were inconvenienced by the fire; however, Princess Cruise line would not commit to paying the cost to send my father home. They acted like his death was unrelated to the fire.

Prior to an autopsy being performed, Princess Cruise line repeatedly and erroneously released information to the media that father died because of a "heart attack." An autopsy was performed by the local medical examiner on March 24, 2006, and the official cause of death was determined to be due to smoke inhalation. Even after the autopsy was completed, Princess Cruise line never issued a statement that listed the correct and official cause of my father's death. Six days after the cruise ship fire, there had been no contact from Princess Cruise line. My father's body was still in Jamaica being held up by red tape. It was not until seven days after this tragic fire, that my father's body was sent home.

My father's death raises larger issues for all of us to consider. Contrary to what the cruise lines suggest, fires present one of the greatest threats to cruise ship safety at sea. For example, in an article entitled "Cruise Ship Fires" written by John Nicholson in the National Fire Protection Association Journal (NFPA), he reports that with bigger and bigger ships being built, the potential for disaster due to ship fires is high, particularly with cruising becoming an increasing popular option for a family vacation.

My father's death was due to a cigarette being flicked overboard (hardly unexpected) which landed on a towel or clothing left on the balcony or the balcony furniture which was combustible. The fire was fueled by the highly combustible material used for partitions on the balconies. Some of the cruise lines replaced the partitions which were obviously fire hazards. However, according to a September 13, 2006, Wall Street Journal article, only 36 ships were being "fixed." The Cruise Line International Association (CLIA) has a total of 24 cruise ship companies with hundreds of cruise ships. Some of the cruise lines have not taken steps to eliminate the danger. The low number of ships being "fixed" reflects that the danger of a fire still exists.

Some of the cruise lines have tried to address the problem by implementing restrictions where passengers can smoke or by implementing "no-smoking" policies. The cruise lines acknowledge that these policies do not work. The practical matter is that each day thousands of passengers still stand by the rails flicking their cigarettes "into the sea." In reality, hundreds of cigarettes are being whipped down into the balconies, where they can be fanned by the wind as the cruise ships sail along at 15 to 20 knots. If the cigarettes come into contact with a towel, the fire can smolder and eventually erupt into a fire. The passengers who sail on the ships do not know which ships have been retrofitted and which ones still have the same type of dangerous partitions and lack balcony smoke/heat detectors and sprinklers. Is this information available to the public? Will CLIA provide it?

Victoria and I met with Princess Cruise line representatives in May of 2007, to find out what changes, if any, had been made to insure that this type of tragedy does not occur again. We were advised that Princess Cruise line retrofitted their balconies with external sprinklers and smoke detectors. This is a responsible first step to protect passengers, and we were encouraged to learn this information. However, we know that other cruise lines have not taken these steps and that CLIA will not do anything to force them to. We are concerned that it is a just a matter of time before another fire occurs.

This is the reason why I joined the ICV, and our family formed a non-profit organization called the "Richard Liffridge Foundation." The foundation was formed to enhance fire safety and regulations on cruise ships. We also created a website, at www.RichardLiffridge.com, to educate the public regarding this danger. By using my father's life as a story, we hope that another family does not experience a similar devastating loss.

The cruise line industry is largely self-regulated and it suffers no real consequences for failing to have comprehensive safety regulations or for not responding quickly in emergency situations. I realize that victims of crime on the cruise ships also experience the same frustrations when cruise lines do not have adequate precautions to protect them from crimes or when they fail to timely and accurately report the crimes. It is important that the ICV continue to act as a watch dog over the cruise lines. We are here asking Congress to enact legislation so that passengers can be safe and the cruise industry can be held accountable when cruise lines act irresponsibly.

During the March 2007 subcommittee hearing, Chairman Cummings made it clear that the cruise lines and the victims need to work together to develop solutions to the current problems facing cruise passengers. Following the hearing; the President of the ICV, Ken Carver, made the initial attempt to schedule a meeting with CLIA. We all knew that Mr. Carver's invitation to the past president of the cruise line trade organization was never accepted or even responded to. The purpose of this renewed effort to meet was to discuss the ICV' s 10 point plan and other suggestions and to review CLIA' s comments regarding each point. The meeting was not held until July 26, 2007, in Washington, DC. As a Board Member of the ICV, I felt that the process to bring CLIA to the table to seriously discuss issues took too long. Many suggestions were made at the meeting regarding how the cruise industry could improve in areas of safety. Although there was some acknowledgment by CLIA that the ICV recommendations were "good ideas," there was no commitment by CLIA to anything in particular and certainly no agreement to legislation. No follow up meeting was scheduled despite our requests.

On August 13 and 14, 2007, CLIA held a meeting where they flew certain victims to Miami and paid for them to stay in hotels and took them out to dinner and so forth. There was no agenda provided by CLIA for the meeting. CLIA solicited primarily victims from the ICV, but told them that their legal representatives were not welcome. CLIA also stated that the media was not welcome. At the end of the meeting, CLIA wanted to form an "advisory committee" where they would pick the members themselves. It is unclear why CLIA wants to have a separate "advisory committee" when there is already an organization formed, ICV, which consists of over 200 members and friends. Our collective "advice" is substantial and the result of years of hard work. Why does CLIA want a hand picked "advisory committee," to be wined and dined again in Miami?

I are concerned that there has been no true progress made since the last hearing. If the cruise industry has committed to changes, they have not shared them with the ICV. Are we going to hear of changes at the hearing for the first time? Our ten point program was presented to the industry over a year ago. Where is the cruise industry's written commitment to specific changes?

This is why it is imperative that legislation be enacted. The cruise industry needs an agency to regulate them. CLIA tells us that by the year 2010, twenty million passengers will sail on CLIA cruise ships. Visions of these passengers flicking their cigarette butts over the rails as unsuspecting passenger are asleep in their cabins, with no fire detectors or sprinklers outside on the balconies, instantly comes to mind. I am sure that the current cruise crime victims fear for the millions of new unsuspecting passengers. Undoubtedly, we will continue to see an increase in the number of crimes and victims while vacationing on cruise ships.

Apparently, the cruise industry is content with a 95-96% satisfaction rate of cruise ships returning safely without incidents. This statement was made by Anita Dunham-Potter on CNBC's "On the Money," which left me with the empty feeling that the cruise industry still "doesn't get it." There are many far too many tragic stories that fall into the remaining 4-5%. When the total number of cruise passengers reaches twenty million a year, this 4-5% turns into 800,000 to 1,000,000 passengers. How many of these passengers will be "dissatisfied' because they are a victim of a crime or a ship fire, or a relative of a missing family member left with no answers?

Please help us enact legislation to protect passengers on cruise ships and hold them accountable when they flaunt reasonable and civilized standard of conduct.

The following are my conclusions regarding my father's cruise, which led to his death and caused injury to his wife:

WHERE THE CRUISE LINE FAILED IN THIS TRAGEDY

- Operating a cruise ship with highly combustible furniture and balcony partitions, with no smoke or heat sensors on the balconies, and failing to have appropriately well trained rescue personnel who could have saved my father after he collapsed in the hallway.
- Not notifying the emergency contact person or any family member.
- Never contacting the family to advise them of the facts surrounding my father's death.
- Failing to commit to pay for the cost of sending my father home.
- Prematurely releasing to the media my father's cause of death as being a "heart attack."
- Improperly releasing my father's medical information.
- Releasing my father's name to the media prior to any family member being notified of his death.

Not only did Princess Cruise line release private information about my father without the family's permission, it provided false medical information to the media which did not relate his death to the fire that killed him.

It was not until October 2006 that our family learned the details surrounding the cause of the fire and the events that led to our father's death. The fire was investigated by the Maritime Accident Investigation Branch (MAIB) which submitted a 52 page report. During the course of the investigation, the MAIB was made aware of six fires on the balconies of cruise ships during which either plastic chairs or beach towels had caught on fire.

Following the fire onboard the Star Princess, a passenger reported that a discarded cigarette had landed on one of the plastic chairs on his balcony and left a burn mark.

Here are some of the areas identified in the MAIB report that contributed to the death of my father:

- The balconies' polycarbonate partitions, polyurethane deck tiles, and the plastic furniture were highly combustible and produced large quantities of very thick black smoke when burned.
- The glass in the doors between the staterooms and balconies were neither fire rated to meet with the requirements of an "A" class division, nor self-closing.
- The balconies crossed main zone fire boundaries, both horizontally and vertically without structural or thermal barriers at the zone or deck boundaries.
- No fire detection or fire suppression systems were fitted on the balconies.
- Access between the balconies was impeded where the keys to the doors in the balcony partitions were not readily available.
- The alleyway doors have a self-closing mechanism. These mechanisms are simultaneously activated when the fire alarm is activated. Some doors were propped open with a wooden wedge. This allowed smoke to reach internal alleyways and accommodation spaces through staterooms via open balcony doors.
- The section leader did not have the master key for certain staterooms which required him to bang on the doors. The section leader was unable to contact the zone commander to inform him about the master key because the telephone lines were busy. This prevented the section leader from informing his zone commander that he had been unable to check the staterooms on the port side of zone 3.
- The ship's medical emergency number was 911. The number was monitored at the customer services desk, which was manned 24 hours per day. The customer services desk was not manned after the crew alert signal was sounded.
- The engine fire party consisted of six members. Five of the party dressed in fire fighting suits and collected their Breathing Apparatus (BA). A sixth member of the BA party had difficulty dressing because his fire suit was too small, and did not collect his BA or the remaining helmet, which contained a thermal imaging camera (TIC). None of the

party wanted to wear this helmet because it was considered to be too heavy and cumbersome.

- The primary language used on most of the radio transmissions was English, although Italian was occasional used between the staff captain and the staff engineer, and the staff engineer and some of his team.
- The probability that passengers were still trapped in zone 3 on deck 12 only became fully apparent when the staff engineer recovered two other passengers (who survived) from the forward end of the alleyway. The engine fire party did not leave its fire locker on deck 4 until about 0324, and proceeded to deck 12 via deck 11 then deck 14. The engine fire party would not have arrived on deck 12, zone 3 until about 0335. By this time, the casualties had been in the alleyway for at least 15 minutes.

It is clear that changes need to be made in the areas of fire safety training, emergency response and in the protocol of handling emergency situations. Without these changes, this type of tragedy will likely occur again.

WHAT CHANGES NEED TO BE MADE

- Smoking needs to be banned or restricted to certain areas of the ship, and enforced.
- Emergency Escape Breathing Devices(EEBD) need to be available for passengers and not only crew members. At least two EEBDs in each cabin on the ships. These devices are economical, and would have saved my dad's life.
- The Death on the High Seas Act needs to be amended to allow recovery for the natural grief and sadness of the surviving family members and the pre-death pain and suffering of my father,
- Fire and security training should be conducted regularly.
- Fire safety instructions should be included in the initial muster drill.
- Fire safety instructions should be placed on the back of the door in each cabin.
- The emergency number should not be unattended or go unanswered at any time during an emergency.

- In an emergency, the first point of contact should be the person listed on the passengers' information sheet.
- The cruise industry should require crew members to attend sensitivity training.
- A team should be formed to assist families during and after a crime or tragedy has occurred on the ship. This team should be the point of contact for the families and should include counselors.

In closing, thank you very much for conducting this important meeting, and listening to my concerns and the comments of others who have been invited here today.

In: Issues in Cruise Ship Safety and Security   ISBN: 978-1-61122-528-0
Editors: Lewis D. Rainer   © 2011 Nova Science Publishers, Inc.

Chapter 9

TESTIMONY OF WILLIAM M. SULLIVAN, JR., ESQ., PARTNER, WINSTON & STRAWN, LLP, WASHINGTON, DC, BEFORE THE SUBCOMMITTEE ON COAST GUARD AND MARITIME TRANSPORTATION

INTRODUCTION

Good [morning/afternoon], Chairman Cummings, Ranking Member LaTourette and Subcommittee members and staff. Thank you for your invitation to address you today about the continued prevalence of sexual assaults against Americans on cruise ships and the willful failure of the cruise industry to institute reasonable security measures, properly respond to sexual assault incidents, care for the victims of these horrific crimes, discourage an onboard culture of reckless profligacy, and warn future passengers of the ongoing danger of rape and sexual assault during cruise vacations.

I am a partner at the law firm of Winston & Strawn LLP, where I specialize in white-collar criminal defense and corporate internal investigations. From 1991-2001, I served as an Assistant United States Attorney for the District of Columbia. In these capacities, I have overseen both criminal investigations and internal corporate investigations, and I have represented corporations and individuals before federal enforcement authorities and regulators, and in criminal and civil litigation. My perspective on the issues addressed by this Subcommittee today has been forged from my experiences both as a prosecutor and as counsel to large corporations. Any way I look at it, the vacation cruise industry is a business in deep trouble.

Last March, Laurie Dishman testified before this Subcommittee and told her heart-wrenching story of how she was raped by a Royal Caribbean employee and was then further victimized by a company that managed its own risk instead of caring for her. Laurie Dishman identified herself as "the next Janet Kelly," relating her story to that of another sexual assault victim who had previously testified before Congress. Laurie Dishman warned that just as she was "the next Janet Kelly" so too would there be a "next Laurie Dishman."

Members of Congress, I represent the next Laurie Dishman, a young American woman who was forcibly raped during what was promoted as a safe vacation experience. Rape is a loathsome crime that has been accurately described as "the murder of the soul." My client is understandably still very shaken by what happened to her and does not wish her identity to be disclosed at this time. To respect her wishes, I will refer to her as Jane Doe throughout my testimony.

What happened to Jane is not an isolated incident. Rather, it persists in an industry that has willfully failed to exercise even the most basic corporate controls despite ample evidence of the dangers to which its passengers are exposed, several reports and recommendations as to how to prevent or minimize those dangers, and its own prior promises to this Congress. I can tell you today that unless cruise lines such as Royal Caribbean drastically change their corporate attitude regarding sexual assaults on their ships, either by their own initiative or as a result of Congressional action, there will be many, many more women victimized like Janet Kelly, Laurie Dishman, and my client, Jane Doe.

JANE DOE'S STORY

Just two weeks before this Subcommittee's March 2007 hearing on cruise ship crime, Jane—a 20-year-old college student—boarded a Royal Caribbean ship with some of her college-age, female friends, to experience the fun and relaxing spring break she saw portrayed in Royal Caribbean's promotional literature. Jane and her friends were led to believe they would be safe onboard the ship, and looked forward to an enjoyable vacation. Midway through the cruise, Jane was brutally raped by her Royal Caribbean cabin steward, who entered a cabin with his Royal Caribbean-issued passkey, after hours, to rape Jane while she slept.

The crewmember who did this was a predator. Earlier that evening, even though he was off duty and had no reason to be near the cabins of Jane and her friends, he imposed himself upon these young women, giving them Royal Caribbean alcohol and encouraging them to consume it with him. During this time, the crewmember watched and lingered as Jane and one of her friends fell sound asleep. Jane's friends escorted him out of the cabin and closed and locked the door behind them before going to their own cabin. Shortly thereafter, the crewmember used his Royal Caribbean passkey to enter the cabin where he knew Jane and her friend lay fast asleep. Without waking Jane or her friend, the crewmember removed Jane's shorts and bikini bottom and forcibly raped her.

Jane awoke as a result of the rape. She struggled to push the rapist off her. She fled the room to seek help. The cabin steward pursued her into the hallway, telling her that nobody would hear her cries for help. She then fled back to the room and slammed the door on him. While Jane and her friend cowered in the cabin, there was a persistent knocking on the door. Because Royal Caribbean's door did not have a peephole, there was no way for Jane and her friend to see who it was. In fact, it was her attacker. Fortunately for Jane, he soon thereafter fled the scene.

Unfortunately, there are no security tapes of the rapist entering the cabin, of Jane attempting to flee her attacker, or of her attacker pursuing her back to the room and persistently knocking on the door. Although corridor security cameras have been a commonplace security feature in hotels around the world for many years, Royal Caribbean has chosen to limit its placement of such equipment to other areas, such as stairwells and lounges. As a Royal Caribbean employee, the rapist plainly knew that his attack would not be observed or recorded by security personnel.

Jane's companions reported the crime immediately by dialing 911 on the ship's phone. The Royal Caribbean employee who answered this call initially did not take the report seriously. In fact, he laughed.

A short time later, Jane was taken to the ship's infirmary, where she expected to receive the urgent medical care and forensic treatment she needed. Instead, she encountered a medical staff whose actions were only to serve Royal Caribbean's risk management interests, at the expense of Jane's medical and emotional needs. The doctor responsible for treating her did not even attempt the most basic procedures consistent with current medical practices that doctors should perform when presented with a rape victim. This doctor did not examine her, did not ask her if there was alcohol or prescription medications in her system, did not perform a rape kit, and did not give her anti-retrovirals and other medications that are so critical when administered properly in preventing HIV and other sexually transmitted diseases.

The only thing that Royal Caribbean's doctor did perform was to fulfill the risk management role assigned to her by Royal Caribbean. Even though Jane was coherent and communicative when she arrived in the infirmary, albeit shaking from the trauma of her rape, the nurse immediately injected Jane with the powerful drug, Lorazepam. Lorazepam is a strong sedative with amnestic properties, tending to cause forgetfulness and to affect memory. Moreover, Lorazepam is known to be dangerous when administered to persons with other medications or alcohol in their systems. Nevertheless, the nurse injected Jane with the drug without even inquiring into her medical history or recent ingestions. Further, Royal Caribbean's nurse did this knowing that Royal Caribbean's doctor would soon compel Jane to make a written statement about the rape, and would be interviewed by local law enforcement.

Indeed, after a short wait for the injection to take effect, the doctor ordered Jane to complete and sign a Royal Caribbean statement form, without informing Jane that the information she provided was not for any medical use, but instead was to be turned over directly to Royal Caribbean's risk management personnel and lawyers. Clearly, such statement form served no legitimate medical purpose, but only served to fulfill Royal Caribbean's risk management purposes and liability defense. Indeed, the doctor provided no medical examination or treatment of Jane whatsoever.

Instead, the doctor abandoned Jane on an infirmary cot for almost six hours, leaving her in a sedated state, in which she was unable to provide meaningful information to local law enforcement. Further, the doctor initially refused the requests of Jane and her companions to call their parents for help and guidance, by telling them that they would have to wait until after the ship sailed from the port.

As a result of Royal Caribbean's doctor's heartless failure to administer anti-retrovirals or rape kit, Jane waited so long before receiving real treatment that she was outside the recommended effective timeframe for receiving these critical medications. Further, the medically and forensically unwarranted passage of time permitted evidence of the rape to deteriorate within and on her body.

The lack of care given in Jane's case extended far beyond the malfeasance of the personnel in the infirmary. Contrary to testimony presented to this Subcommittee in March, Royal Caribbean did not assign the most-senior female officer to serve as Jane's advocate. Rather, Royal Caribbean left Jane and her friends to fend for themselves amid foreign law enforcement personnel and Royal Caribbean employees whose actions were directed exclusively to protecting the company's liability interests.

Royal Caribbean ultimately abandoned Jane at the foreign port of call to the local authorities. The company refused to provide accommodations to permit her traveling companions to remain with her, so Jane and one friend stayed behind while the rest of their group left with the ship. Since Jane had received no actual medical treatment onboard and no rape kit had been performed, the local police took her to a hospital emergency room, which, ironically, was only minutes away from the ship. However, because Royal Caribbean failed to make any provisions for taking Jane to the best possible facility in the city—even though it was virtually the same distance from the port—the police took her to the local public hospital. As a result, Jane was not treated until many hours after she should have been, and then received substandard care. Among other things, she did not receive the anti-retrovirals she needed to minimize the risk of HIV infection until at least six hours later, and even then, she received only half of the standard dosage of these anti-retrovirals which she should have received, and would have received, at any reputable emergency room in the United States.

Even after Jane left the ship, Royal Caribbean continued its risk management tactics. Witnesses have reported that Royal Caribbean failed to properly secure the crime scene such that unauthorized individuals had easy access to it.

Royal Caribbean also failed to consider the needs of Jane's traveling companions, who remained on the ship until the father of one of Jane's friends contacted law enforcement in the United States and informed them that his daughter did not feel safe onboard. Upon receiving this chapter, the ship's staff captain pressured the young woman to retract her statement, and to say that she was fine. Of course, she was not fine. These young women were all traumatized by what had happened, and they had virtually no information regarding Jane's condition or well-being.

Meanwhile, as Jane was traveling back to the United States from the foreign port, she received persistent calls on her cell phone from an individual in Royal Caribbean's "guest care" department. This person insistently pressured her to accept counseling with a therapist associated with Royal Caribbean—whose employee had just raped her—and continued to harass Jane even after she declined. Through correspondence with Royal Caribbean, it later became clear that Jane's instincts were correct. Just like the doctor onboard the ship, this purported "guest care" person was part of Royal Caribbean's risk management operation. She took notes regarding her calls with Jane and passed on a distorted account of these conversations to Royal Caribbean's lawyers.

Surprisingly—and this is unusual because it is apparently extremely rare even though cruise ships are controlled environments that cannot be easily fled—Jane's rapist was apprehended by local authorities, is currently incarcerated, and will stand trial. Despite this, Royal Caribbean still refuses to provide Jane either the basic information necessary for her continuing medical care, or the evidence it retains that is needed to bring Jane's rapist to justice. For example, even though U.S. privacy laws do not apply to foreign cruise line employees, Jane still has not received her rapist's Royal Caribbean medical records. As a result, she is forced to live daily with the dread that the half-dosage of anti-retrovirals and other medications she received many hours too late will prove insufficient to protect her from HIV and any other sexually transmitted diseases her rapist may have had.

Additionally, Royal Caribbean has refused to share with Jane or the local prosecutors the non-privileged statements it obtained from the rapist during repeated visits to him in the foreign prison.

Royal Caribbean had a duty to Jane Doe, as it had a duty to Laurie Dishman and Janet Kelly before her. It betrayed that duty when it gave a rapist unrestricted access to her and her cabin, when it injected her with a dangerous drug to inhibit her ability to report her attack, and when it failed to provide the medications she needed to prevent HIV infection, and it continues to betray her as it fails to support her efforts to see the rapist brought to justice.

ROYAL CARIBBEAN'S TRACK RECORD

Jane's experience is far from unique. Royal Caribbean was able to execute its well-orchestrated risk management plan because it deals with these situations frequently. In my experience, corporations that uncover problems within their organizations have two options: 1) they can admit there is a problem and take immediate short- and long-term steps to address it; or 2) they can do nothing and act to hide the problem.

Royal Caribbean seems to believe that since these crimes occur far away from the eyes of the news media and U.S. law enforcement personnel, it sails with impunity and can get away with failing to take reasonable preventative measures, failing to report sexual assaults, tampering with witnesses, contaminating crime scenes and allowing them to deteriorate, and continuing to misrepresent the risks of sexual assault to which it exposes the U.S. citizens who pay money to vacation onboard its ships.

The problem is that with every warning Royal Caribbean fails to heed, victims like Jane pay the price. And Royal Caribbean has received plenty of warnings. The company has known for years that sexual assaults are a problem on its ships. In the past several years alone, Royal Caribbean ships have been the scene of hundreds of reported sexual assaults, many by Royal Caribbean employees.[1] Indeed, in Jane's case, the specific Royal Caribbean personnel onboard had prior personal experience responding to a reported sexual assault. Mr. Crisologo Dionaldo, who served as head of security on Jane's vessel, also was the head of security on Laurie Dishman's ship when she was brutally raped by a Royal Caribbean employee.

In May 1999, Royal Caribbean hired a consulting company, The Krohne Connection, to prepare a report regarding the problem with sexual assaults on its cruise ships. The report concluded that "improper activity occurs frequently aboard ships, but goes unreported and/or unpunished." In June 1999, another consulting company hired by Royal Caribbean, Swailes, Sheridan, Slade & Associates, presented a study to the company entitled "Reducing Sexual Assaults on Cruise Ships: Risk Assessment and Recommendations." This study concluded that "crew members generally understand that if they commit an offense and are caught they are most likely going to lose their job and be returned home, but not spend time in jail." These consulting firms recommended concrete steps Royal Caribbean could take to reduce the number of sexual assaults on its ships. I am presently unaware as to whether Royal Caribbean has altered its written policies in response to these recommendations, although I intend to find out. I can tell you that, based on Jane's experience, these changes have not been implemented in practice, even though the company received these reports eight years ago.

RECOMMENDATIONS FOR IMPROVEMENT

There are many things Royal Caribbean and other cruise lines could and should do to prevent sexual assaults and—when these crimes occur—to properly investigate them and care for their victims. Most of these ideas are not new or particularly innovative. They have been recommended to the cruise lines by their own consultants, by past victims and by members of Congress. They have been used by the hotel industry and other tourism-based industries for years, which have found them to be both successful and cost-effective. Despite the many pleas for improvements, the practical recommendations, and the proven track record of such actions, the cruise line industry has not implemented these changes. I am here today in the hope that a combination of public and Congressional pressure will finally force Royal Caribbean and other cruise lines to do what they should have done years ago to prevent and properly respond to these horrible crimes.

At a minimum, cruise lines should:

- Institute passkey technologies and/or controls to prevent crew members from using passkeys when off duty, and to effectively monitor crewmembers who are entering passenger cabins in the course of their duties. This is necessary in view of the increased risk posed by cabin stewards who have easy and frequent access to passengers, as noted in Royal Caribbean's June 1999 Swailes study. The technology is already well-established, and control procedures can easily be implemented to restrict the use of passkeys to certain hours or to establish a system whereby crew members physically turn in passkeys when they go off duty.

- Install peepholes and chains for all cabin doors.

- Install and monitor security cameras in the hallways of passenger cabins. This security method is routine throughout the hotel industry. Indeed, Royal Caribbean stated at the March hearing that it is changing to a digital security camera system. However, updated cameras are useless if they are not placed—and monitored—in ship areas where activity precedent to sexual assault commonly occurs. In Jane's case, had there been a monitored camera in her hallway, the rapist would likely have been deterred from committing the attack, and if not, security would have seen her rapist enter her cabin twice during a time period when he was off duty, and would have seen him pursuing her as she attempted to flee.

- Create a guest care team that lives up to its name. Ensure that guest care team members are independent of the corporate risk management department and outside counsel, and do not communicate information regarding a cruise line victim without the victim's written authorization. Provide training for guest care team members as to appropriate ways to assist victims of violent crime.

- Record all shipboard 911 calls. In an environment where there are no U.S. law enforcement authorities to whom passengers may turn when victimized by shipboard crime, the cruise lines must at the very least record their passengers' pleas for help.
- Ensure that all ships carry adequate supplies of rape kits, anti-retrovirals and other medications used to prevent STDs after a sexual assault, and administer a rape kit and anti-retroviral medications onboard if a rape victim cannot be transported to an adequate medical facility immediately after the rape. Notably, in Jane's case, there was a rape kit onboard, but Royal Caribbean chose not to use it. Although I do not know if the ship had anti-retrovirals and other appropriate medications onboard, given Royal Caribbean's track record of sex assaults onboard, it should have maintained such items.
- Provide all sexual assault victims with the medical records of their rapists, so that victims may be properly treated for HIV and any other sexually transmitted diseases. (The cruise lines regularly assert that they are not covered by U.S. laws such as HIPAA, so crewmembers accused of rape are not entitled to medical records privacy.)
- Warn passengers that cruise ships are not crime-free. Cruise lines conduct safety drills at the beginning of each cruise during which passengers are taught where their life preservers are located and how to find their muster stations in case of emergency. Cruise lines also regularly warn passengers to beware of crime in certain ports of call. However, ship personnel fail to caution passengers about onboard crime. Cruise ships should warn passengers in writing and orally that they must be just as cautious on the ship as they would be in any city environment.
- Perform reasonable background checks on all employees who will be given unrestricted or unsupervised access to passengers, and provide appropriate supervision. In Jane's case, Royal Caribbean assigned a young man to be the cabin steward for a number of college-age women on a spring-break vacation cruise, and gave him unrestricted access to their rooms, apparently without any supervision or monitoring to ensure that he did not prey upon them.
- Immediately notify the FBI if a crime occurs involving a U.S. citizen. Royal Caribbean has previously testified that this is the company's policy, but in Jane's case the FBI was not notified until approximately 12 hours after the crime.

Anyone who suggests the industry can't afford these changes hasn't looked at the profit margins. Royal Caribbean is a $14 billion company that made $634 million in profits last year alone. As a company organized under the laws of Liberia, it does not pay the same U.S. taxes that other companies do. The cost of these improvements is pocket change for such a successful enterprise.

Indeed, in the long run, these changes will save the company money. If Royal Caribbean and other cruise lines fail to upgrade their policies, procedures and security operations, they will see an ever-growing number of victims prepared to file suits for damages based both on the company's strict liability for its employees' crimes, and on the company's own intentional misconduct in failing to prevent these incidents. The cruise industry also will see an increasingly educated customer base choosing to forgo the risks of a cruise vacation where they will be at the mercy of foreign-flag ships and their employees who believe themselves to be beyond the reach of the law. Making the recommended changes will be inexpensive in comparison, and it will also allow the industry to honestly portray itself to future customers as a relatively safe and enjoyable vacation opportunity.

CONCLUSION

Because of the nature of the cruise industry, victims come from all parts of the country and all walks of life. Royal Caribbean alone had more than 10 million passengers last year. Unless real changes are implemented, and soon, any one of our loved ones could become the next "Jane Doe," savaged first by the depraved conduct of a crewmember, and then brutalized again by the unconscionable acts of a company determined to protect its public image and pocketbook without regard to the personal cost to its passengers.

I understand that our society is not crime-free and that cruise ships likely cannot be either. The critical question is whether the cruise industry is doing everything reasonable to prevent these horrific crimes of rape and sexual assault, and is responding in a responsible and appropriate manner when such crimes do occur.

Based on my client's experience, my survey of similar industries, and my experiences both as a former federal prosecutor and as a private lawyer conducting internal investigations, I believe the cruise industry is capable of much, much more. The industry owes its passengers safety and respect, not the callous, arrogant attitude that allows onboard sexual assault to be a chronic, unaddressed problem.

It is apparent that despite the cruise line industry's existing common law and statutory obligations, these companies are not willing to implement the security and response measures necessary to safeguard American citizen passengers from the very real threat of sexual assault and other violent crimes. Congress has acted before to prevent cruise lines from avoiding liability for the sexual assaults committed by its employees,[2] but unfortunately that has not been enough. I request and encourage this Congress to further protect American citizen passengers through legislation requiring passenger vessel security plans to specifically address the risk of assaults on cruise ships and through federal codification of heightened liability against cruise lines that fail to take adequate measures to protect their passengers. Without such action, cruise lines will continue to view the victimization of American citizens as merely the cost of doing business.

Thank you. I look forward to your questions.

End Notes

[1] Kimi Yoshino, *Cruise industry's dark waters; What happens at sea stays there as crimes on liners go unresolved*, Los Angeles Times, Jan. 20, 2007.

[2] 46 U.S.C. § 30509(b)(2).

In: Issues in Cruise Ship Safety and Security   ISBN: 978-1-61122-528-0
Editors: Lewis D. Rainer   © 2011 Nova Science Publishers, Inc.

Chapter 10

TESTIMONY OF GARY M. BALD, SENIOR VICE PRESIDENT OF GLOBAL SECURITY, ROYAL CARIBBEAN CRUISES LTD., BEFORE THE SUBCOMMITTEE ON COAST GUARD AND MARITIME TRANSPORTATION

Good morning, Mr. Chairman, Congressman LaTourette, and Members of the Subcommittee. I would like to take this opportunity to thank you, Mr. Chairman, and the Subcommittee, for holding these hearings. Thank you for your invitation to address you today about the continued prevalence of sexual assaults against Americans on cruise ships and the willful failure of the cruise industry to institute reasonable security measures, properly respond to sexual assault incidents, care for the victims of these horrific crimes, discourage an onboard culture of reckless profligacy, and warn future passengers of the ongoing danger of rape and sexual assault during cruise vacations.

I first appeared before the Subcommittee in March of this year at which time I had served just nine months as the head of global security for the Royal Caribbean cruise brands, which include: Royal Caribbean International, Celebrity Cruises and Azamara Cruises. At that time, Mr. Chairman, I testified to a number of shortcomings in our policies and procedures which, unfortunately, led to additional trauma for several guests who had suffered a crisis while on vacation with us. I also testified about some of the changes we had put into place to address these shortcomings. Those changes remain in place and are part of a strategy to advance our security to ensure the welfare of our guests.

GUEST SECURITY STRATEGY

At Royal Caribbean, our guest security strategy is to implement processes that prevent and effectively respond to security incidents. Prevention, our highest priority, is being pursued through a dual effort of 1) effective deterrence, and 2) understanding and eliminating the factors that contribute to incidents. Simply stated, I believe that if we can eliminate the factors that lead to incidents, we will be able to prevent incidents from occurring.

In those situations where an incident does occur, our goal is to effectively respond in a manner that restores safety and security; treats and cares for our guest appropriately and with compassion; identifies those responsible; preserves evidence; and facilitates and supports investigation of the incident and prosecution of those responsible.

The first steps in this process are underway. We have instituted a deterrent presence on several of our ships, and will expand this in the future. The next step involves developing a process to identify the factors that contribute to incidents. Once this step is complete, we will begin to collect and evaluate this information and develop security measures that eliminate these contributing factors.

In the mean time, we are redefining the roles and qualifications of our security staff and providing the training they need to be successful. We have revised several of our key processes, and expect to eventually conclude a complete rewrite of our security procedures. We are aggressively re-training our security teams on how to recognize and preserve evidence; how to conduct post-incident follow-up; and, importantly, on the acceptable manner in which to interact with victims of crimes.

Although I will list below some of the steps we have already taken, there are many others, both underway and planned, that I can not present today in this open setting. Some of these fall into the categories of security countermeasures; promising proprietary technical research and development; and personnel initiatives. It is important to note that although I believe we have come a long way in our security efforts, we still have much more to accomplish. Ultimately, this process is not about statistics or even about past incidents, although both are important. It is about preventing even a single negative experience on a cruise ship. This is no small task. With the continual support of this Committee, government officials, our cruise industry counterparts and our incident-survivor partners, I am confident our efforts will make a significant impact on the issues we collectively face and on the cruise experiences of our future guests.

EXTERNAL INPUT AND RECOMMENDATIONS

Since the March hearing before this Committee, I have benefited from both direct and indirect input from cruise incident survivors. Their unique perspectives have afforded me an excellent compass-check to ensure my efforts are on a course that will prevent future incidents. Many of the suggestions I have received from survivors have either led to new initiatives; validated current projects; or produced promising ideas for future planning. We have also received recommendations from the International Cruise Victims Association. Their "Ten-Point Program" contains sound concepts and, although in some instances we do not agree with their implementation approach, their work has stimulated productive dialogue. In general, their proposals are consistent with our goals to ensure: reliable cruise employee vetting; well-trained and capable shipboard security with a high degree of integrity and appropriate oversight; effective video surveillance systems; viable technology and processes to address missing persons; and capable medical care. I am also particularly pleased and optimistic about CLIA's initiative to form a Survivor/Industry Working Group. Based on what I know about the survivors who have volunteered to serve on this group, I am confident that we will continue to make progress through this collaborative process and the flow of security ideas for the future will be rich and well informed.

SECURITY PROGRESS

Today, I am pleased to report that we have continued to make progress in both securing our ships and in providing needed personal and emotional support to our guests. Mr. Chairman, as I have noted, our progress over the last six months has been greatly enhanced by the partnership of cruise incident survivors who have graciously provided firsthand accounts of ways in which we can improve. I have spent many hours in personal discussions and reviewing input from incident survivors and their families. I have found the information I have received to be very helpful in ensuring the direction of my improvement strategies is in keeping with the needs of those I am dedicated to protect.

For the past several years, Royal Caribbean has focused on improving the tools, technology, training, and performance of our company in terms of security and guest care. Although I would be pleased to respond to questions about any of the initiatives we have undertaken, for purposes of my remarks today, I would like to focus on some of the steps we have taken in the six months that have passed since this subcommittee's last hearing in late March of this year. The majority of these steps in our ongoing security progress speak to issues raised in our conversations with individual incident survivors and in the written proposals for improvement we have received.

April 2007

- At the conclusion of the March 27, 2007 hearing, I was approached by Kimberly Edwards, a cruise incident survivor. Ms. Edwards expressed concern over her personal cruise experience and manner in which her situation was handled. I addressed her concern and we began a dialogue about shipboard security that has been very informative. I found Ms. Edwards to be a strong advocate of her own and other cruise victims' concerns and someone with the ability to bridge perspective gaps such as those that may develop between the industry and incident survivors. The manner in which she has approached our mutual goal of security improvements confirmed for me the absolute need to involve survivors in our security improvement process.
- We have entered into a partnership with the Rape Assault and Incest National Network (RAINN). RAINN, the nation's largest anti-sexual assault organization, operates a National Sexual Assault Hotline, and conducts programs to prevent sexual assault, help victims, and ensure that perpetrators are brought to justice. We are working with RAINN to establish access from our ships to RAINN's web-based 24-hour Online Hotline and to their 24-hour 800 Telephone Hotline for those rare instances where a guest or crew member becomes the victim of a sexual assault. Our mutual goal is to facilitate both immediate and continuing professional counseling services should a guest desire and need this assistance. Our partnership with RAINN will contribute strongly to the support now routinely provided to guests by Royal Caribbean's Guest Care Team.
- After meeting Ken Carver for the first time at the March hearing, we began an exchange of information concerning his daughter's apparent suicide, as well as information about the International Cruise Victims Association's (ICVA) recommendations for security improvements.

Through CLIA's leadership, I look forward to continuing discussions with Mr. Carver as we advance our efforts to address our mutual concerns.

- We began a formalized process whereby the Global Security Department and the Risk Management Department of Royal Caribbean conduct formal quarterly reviews of all shipboard incidents. This is an oversight process that helps us ensure incidents are properly reported, characterized and addressed at various levels/perspectives and offers an additional opportunity to identify lessons learned and areas where we can improve.

- We implemented a Guest Care checklist for ships' management to facilitate consistent support of our guests' emotional and logistical needs following an unforeseen event. This includes providing shipboard toll free telephone access for guests to RAINN, the FBI and other law enforcement entities who may be involved in responding to their shipboard incident. This is a service that will be routinely provided under the Royal Caribbean Guest Care Program.

May 2007

- Laurie Dishman, who testified on the victim's panel at the March 27, 2007 hearing, and I exchanged several emails which included her thoughtful suggestions for security improvements. Although our interactions have been limited by her attorney's concerns about pending litigation, Ms. Dishman's suggestions have directly led to security improvements within Royal Caribbean. I hope one day to discuss our security initiatives with Ms. Dishman and to obtain more of her valuable input and feedback.

- Royal Caribbean co-sponsored a Family Assistance Foundation (FAF) symposium in Atlanta, Georgia. The symposium was attended by survivors and industry representatives and was facilitated by Dr. Carolyn Coarsey of the FAF. The conference successfully enabled all parties to discuss our shared goal of enhancing transportation security while at the same time providing a much needed opportunity for us to interact on a personal level with persons who are survivors of a cruise-related incident. The value of these discussions has been evident in the progress the industry has made in addressing survivors' specific concerns.

- We implemented a formal "after-action process" at the conclusion of the internal handling of a shipboard incident involving a sexual assault or a "man-overboard" incident. While we do many things right, we have learned from our survivors that there are things we have done wrong or that we could do better in these matters. For that reason, we have designed the after-action review process to identify lessons learned and to make appropriate improvements.
- We formed an internal Employee Vetting Working Group to re-evaluate both our internal and outsourced vetting processes and to identify opportunities for improvement. This group will also further explore legal ways to address the vetting concerns expressed by Ms. Dishman and the ICVA.

June 2007

- We entered into an agreement with an outside contractor to supply former federal, state and local law enforcement investigative experts who are on call to respond to certain ship-board incidents such as man overboard or sexual assault incidents. This team provides us a resource we can dispatch with strong investigative credentials to assist in understanding how an incident occurred and what steps we can take to prevent a recurrence. Given the input we have received from this committee and our survivors, we have required this team to include highly skilled female investigators who will greatly add to our efforts to effectively respond, assess and ultimately prevent sexual assault incidents.

July 2007

- We expanded our existing internal Watchlisting Process to include all terminated Royal Caribbean employees. This now permits us to consider whether a terminated employee should be permitted to sail as a guest on a Royal Caribbean ship in the future. Existing protocols within the Human Resources Department already ensure that a terminated employee will not be rehired without a complete review of the reasons for a prior termination. Terminations for criminal activity are a bar against both sailing with and future employment with Royal Caribbean. (Due to prohibitions on the practice of blacklisting, within the context of anti-discrimination laws, civil rights laws, antitrust laws and labor laws, Royal Caribbean does not share a list of employees terminated for criminal activity with other cruise lines, as has been recommended by the International Cruise Victims Association.)

- We contracted with an outside expert for the development of incident metrics to facilitate a prevention approach to shipboard security. The goal of this project is to identify and eliminate patterns in circumstances that contribute to shipboard incidents. If we can better understand the underlying causes of incidents, we will be better able to target them for elimination.

- We added two new full-time employees to our Guest Care Team, bringing this important response team to a total of five full-time specialists prepared to travel on a moment's notice anywhere in the world when an RCL guests needs assistance. This team, lead by a registered nurse, has received amazing results and feedback from those they have helped.

- We filled the first position on our Global Security Department's investigative team. This 20 year veteran and Detective from the New York City Police Department brings extensive investigative experience to the department. (See the August entry below for more details on the role of this team.)

- We participated with CLIA and other cruise industry colleagues in a meeting with several board members of the International Cruise Victims Association to discuss suggestions for improving ship security. We believe continuing dialogue with the survivors of cruise incidents will permit us to match improvement processes to some of the concepts underlying the ICVA's Ten-Point program for the benefit of all cruise travelers.

- We formally established security career path and related job descriptions for our shipboard security teams. This is the first of several steps we will take to ensure we attract and retain high-quality, motivated professionals to these critical positions.

August 2007

- We joined CLIA, other cruise industry colleagues and the Family Assistance Foundation in meeting with survivors and family members of incidents on cruise ships. This meeting was to permit us to hear directly from survivors suggestions for improving the security and guest care practices of the industry in ways that will help us prevent future incidents. This meeting was very productive and produced ideas and partnerships that bode well for future guests and the industry on topics such as prevention, training, guest care, family support, communication and medical care. Survivors expressed their desire to participate in a formal working group with the industry. This working group is being formed by CLIA and will provide further opportunities to continue this great exchange.

- We developed a plan for the installation of peep holes in guest stateroom cabins on an existing ship in October 2007. This follows an earlier decision to install peep holes in guest staterooms on two ships currently being built. We are in the process of obtaining fire safety acceptance for our proposed installation process from Det Norske Veritas, the classification society for technical requirements for construction or design and certifications for industry standards. Pending this certification of our process, installation will proceed in October, and planning to install peep holes on all Royal Caribbean ships will move forward. This initiative is the result of a suggestion from Laurie Dishman, and is further evidence of the value of our ongoing dialogue with cruise incident survivors.

- To ensure our shipboard executives understand the impact our handling of incidents has on our guests, we distributed a DVD containing excerpts from the March 2007 Congressional Hearing of this Subcommittee to every ship in the fleet. This DVD is now mandatory viewing for Captains, Staff Captains, Hotel Directors, Security Officers, Security Staff, Medical Staff and Guest Services Desk Staff. The DVD highlights testimony from survivors expressing the trauma they experienced; government witnesses setting forth their role in investigating incidents onboard cruise ships; and Members of the Subcommittee, including the Chairman, expressing their commitment to seeing improvement in the security and care of the cruising public.

- We formally amended policy on incident response and codified these changes in Royal Caribbean manuals. This new policy reflects our emphasis on preserving evidence and standardized the method by which we will reliably secure staterooms that become the location of a shipboard incident.
- We hired two additional experienced investigators, both women, as full-time members of the Global Security Department's investigative team. These career professionals, along with their counterpart hired in July and their Director, bring over 80 years of investigative experience to the company, and form a team whose past assignments include the handling of sexual assault investigations and strong experience working with international law enforcement partners. They will directly oversee our response to shipboard incidents; ensure the complete reporting of criminal incidents to the appropriate law enforcement agency (worldwide); and direct the response of contract investigators when needed. This team is also joined by a newly hired senior intelligence analyst, with U.S. Intelligence Community experience, to monitor changes in world security risks and drive appropriate corporate response.
- To further elevate the importance of shipboard security, the Chairman and CEO of Royal Caribbean Cruises Ltd. approved that I, as Senior Vice President for Global Security, participate in evaluating the annual performance of our shipboard Captains. This is the process that determines their end of year bonus. This supplements the role I play in the annual ratings of Staff Captains and Security Officers.

September 2007

- We formally reassigned accountability for our response to shipboard criminal incidents and man overboard investigations from the Risk Management Department to the Global Security Department. This places day-to-day planning, response, reporting and oversight for incidents in the hands of career investigative professionals.
- Our next generation SeaPass Program entered the Request-for-Proposal Phase. This will provide our ships with a platform-based guest identification and purchasing card with enhanced security recognition features. This approach will also provide opportunities to

leverage anticipated near-term technology advancements as they become available.

- We began including the FBI in our quarterly reviews of shipboard incidents by the Global Security Department and the Risk Management Department. This provides valuable input and an additional level of oversight to our incident handling and reporting process.

- The Family Assistance Foundation provided training to Royal Caribbean corporate communication and security officials focusing on the importance of effectively communicating with guests and their families, with employees, and with the public in the event of an incident. The FAF also shared videotaped interviews of survivors who described the positive impact on their emotional recovery of cruise employees who responded immediately and appropriately to their needs.

- We developed and submitted for publication, a concise safety/security guide for guests. This guide, to appear on the inside cover of every guest stateroom service directory in the Royal Caribbean, Celebrity and Azamara fleet, includes shipboard emergency contact numbers, safety/security tips and other helpful security information. This step is the result of a specific recommendation of Kimberly Edwards, a cruise incident survivor who has graciously shared her time to help improve cruise ship security.

- To ensure that shipboard medical staff are familiar with the proper procedures for administering the Pelvic Examination Kit, we forwarded a supplemental training DVD to each ship for mandatory viewing by all medical staff members. This is an initiative recommended by this committee in March of this year.

- We formally established that only full-time security crew members may carry or display a security badge. This will help guests distinguish between our onboard security professionals from other members of the crew.

- Finally, next week, we will provide our annual Security Officers training seminar. This year, we will include presentations by the Family Assistance Foundation, in addition to our many technical and procedural sessions and FBI training. During this ten-day session, Security Officers will receive presentations on topics such as incident reporting requirements, incident prevention, incident response, evidence preservation, conflict resolution, guest care, victim concerns, intelligence, terrorism and security countermeasures. This training will also result in each Security Officer training and then sitting for his Security Industry Authority (SIA) License, as taught, regulated and issued by the United Kingdom.

Incident Reporting

Before concluding my statement, Mr. Chairman, I would like to mention that the cruise industry's standardized reporting agreement with the FBI and Coast Guard has been in place now for six months and, from Royal Caribbean's perspective, has been fully and successfully implemented. Between the time of the last hearing and September 1, 2007, my team has worked in partnership with our Risk Management Department to ensure our reporting requirements are being met. As I indicated earlier in my written statement, effective September 1, 2007, I became personally responsible for ensuring that all criminal incidents are appropriately reported. I pledge to you that I will continue the commitment to full reporting that our CEO mandated several years ago and that I will ensure our processes and actions result in our meeting both the letter and spirit of our agreement with the FBI and the U.S. Coast Guard.

I want to make one thing very clear about our reporting obligations. It is my understanding that the reporting standards in the industry/FBI-USCG agreement are required by U.S. law and/or regulations. I base this understanding on information from industry and corporate legal guidance as well as from information provided by the FBI and U.S. Coast Guard. Nothing I have heard or reviewed would permit me to follow any other course. However, regardless of others' interpretations of our legal reporting obligations, the instructions I have given to my team are clear. Our ships will promptly report ALL crimes on board our ships to my department; and my department will report or ensure reporting of shipboard crimes to the appropriate authorities immediately upon receipt. This is not only the right thing to do, it is an integral part of my efforts to understand shipboard incidents and develop prevention strategies.

CONCLUSION

Mr. Chairman, at Royal Caribbean, we are committed to providing an exceptional and safe vacation experience for our guests. If a guest becomes the victim of a crime, we want to ensure that they and their family members or traveling companions are appropriately cared for; that the person(s) responsible are effectively investigated; and that steps are taken to learn from and prevent the incident from happening again. To reach that goal, we will continue to work in partnership with survivors and their families; with outside experts such as the Family Assistance Foundation and RAINN; and with the federal government. I am personally committed to keeping open the lines of communication with these important partners and to provide periodic updates to you Mr. Chairman and other Members of the Subcommittee, as desired.

Thank you again for the opportunity to be here today. I am happy to respond to any questions you may have.

CHAPTER SOURCES

The following chapters have been previously published:

Chapter 1 – This is an edited, excerpted and augmented edition of a United States Government Accountability Office publication, Report Order Code GAO-10-400, dated April 2010.

Chapter 2 – These remarks were delivered as Statement of Terry Dale, before the United States Senate Committee on Commerce, Science and Transportation, given June 19, 2008.

Chapter 3 – These remarks were delivered as Testimony of Evelyn Fortier, before the United States Senate Committee on Commerce, Science and Transportation, given June 19, 2008.

Chapter 4 – These remarks were delivered as Testimony of Ross A. Klein, PhD, before the United States Senate Committee on Commerce, Science and Transportation, given June 19, 2008.

Chapter 5 – This is an edited, excerpted and augmented edition of a United States House of Representatives Committee on Transportation and Infrastructure Hearing on Cruise Ship Security Practices and Procedures, given September 17, 2007.

Chapter 6 – These remarks were delivered as Statement of Rear Admiral Wayne Justice, before the U.S. House of Representatives Committee on Transportation and Infrastructure, given September 19, 2007.

Chapter 7 – These remarks were delivered as Statement of Salvatore Hernandez, before the U.S. House of Representatives Committee on Transportation and Infrastructure, given September 19, 2007.

Chapter 8 – These remarks were delivered as Testimony of Lynette Hudson, before the U.S. House of Representatives Committee on Transportation and Infrastructure, given September 19, 2007.

Chapter 9 – These remarks were delivered as Testimony of William M. Sullivan, Jr., Esq., before the U.S. House of Representatives Committee on Transportation and Infrastructure, given September 19, 2007.

Chapter 10 – These remarks were delivered as Statement of Gary M. Bald, before the U.S. House of Representatives Committee on Transportation and Infrastructure, given September 19, 2007.

INDEX

blood, 97
board members, 149
Border Patrol, 8
border search, 10
border security, 2, 4
breakdown, 107, 116
bribes, 83
burn, 128
business model, 94
business partners, vii, 49
businesses, viii, 49, 70

C

Caribbean, 8, 40, 42, 55, 65, 77, 78, 83, 84,
 85, 91, 96, 97, 99, 101, 132, 133, 134,
 135, 136, 137, 138, 139, 140, 143, 144,
 145, 146, 147, 148, 150, 151, 152, 153,
 154
Carnival Cruise Lines, 65, 82, 83, 84
cash, 117
category a, 117
cell phones, 52
certification, 150
CFR, ix, 86, 98, 112, 115
challenges, 31, 85
Chamber of Commerce, 55, 66
childhood, viii, 69
children, 79, 87
citizens, ix, 69, 70, 78, 86, 99, 111, 113,
 114, 137, 141
citizenship, 45
City, 8, 67, 149
civil liberties, 34
civil rights, 149
class, 42, 128
classification, 117, 150
cleaning, 82, 90, 97
CLIA, viii, ix, 49, 50, 51, 61, 65, 91, 93, 98,
 100, 103, 105, 106, 107, 108, 113, 115,
 116, 117, 118, 124, 125, 126, 145, 147,
 149, 150
clients, 75, 77
clothing, 54, 124
CNN, 123
Code of Federal Regulations, ix, 104, 115

commerce, 4
commercial, viii, 25, 81, 99
common law, 141
communication, 150, 152, 154
communities, 46, 77
community, 27, 32, 77
compassion, 50, 144
complaints, 75, 83
compliance, 9, 10, 15, 44, 45, 108, 113
computer, 61
conference, 32, 147
conflict, 72, 152
conflict of interest, 72
conflict resolution, 152
Congress, 16, 39, 69, 76, 78, 90, 97, 98,
 125, 132, 138, 141
Congressional Budget Office, 4
connectivity, 34
consciousness, 123
consent, 44, 73
construction, 150
consulting, 61, 137
consumers, 70, 114
consumption, 94
contamination, 21
control measures, 28
conversations, 136, 146
cooperation, 27, 32, 73
coordination, ix, 27, 30, 45, 112, 116
cost, 3, 32, 33, 34, 35, 37, 124, 127, 138,
 140, 141
counsel, 53, 132, 138
counseling, 71, 77, 135, 146
credentials, 148
crew, vii, 3, 4, 9, 10, 14, 20, 24, 25, 33, 44,
 45, 50, 52, 53, 73, 77, 78, 81, 84, 85, 86,
 90, 91, 92, 93, 94, 95, 97, 99, 104, 122,
 128, 129, 130, 137, 138, 146, 152
crimes, viii, ix, x, 52, 53, 73, 75, 76, 78, 84,
 86, 87, 95, 98, 99, 103, 104, 105, 106,
 108, 111, 112, 113, 118, 119, 121, 125,
 126, 131, 136, 137, 140, 141, 143, 144,
 153
criminal activity, 53, 106, 148
criminal acts, 43